Nice To Meet You!
Now What?

LIZ GARANT

ISBN-10: 1546979212
ISBN-13: 978-1546979210

CONTENTS

ACKNOWLEDGMENTS

Many thanks to Angela Sealana for her generous efforts in providing feedback during the final editing process and to Cathy Shaffer for her feedback while reviewing the first draft.

Thanks also to my first ministry partners who inspired me and helped to shape my desire to write this book. Gabe Ruiz who was quick to befriend and encourage me when I arrived at the St Mary Magdalen Young Adult Group. Kristin Sanchez whose willingness to serve others and fierce love for the truth made her an invaluable partner and friend during the many ministry adventures we shared.

Many thanks also to my parents, whose love and support over the years helped lay the foundation for my faith.

INTRODUCTION

How well do you know Jesus?

Maybe you've heard a lot about Him. Maybe you even make a point of going to church, reading your Bible, or praying regularly. These are good things. We can do all of these things, though, and still end up in a place where we know a lot about Jesus but we don't actually know Jesus Himself very well. It's the same thing which happens with celebrities: we know lots about them but we don't know them personally.

Maybe Jesus isn't just someone you know a lot about but someone you've met in a personal way. There was that awesome time (maybe you were on a retreat) where you felt you were meeting God in a new way. Maybe that experience really lit your faith on fire but that was some time ago and you haven't felt that way since. Now you just kind of go through the motions while waiting for that next experience to come around and kick start your spiritual life again.

Or maybe you've reached a place where you know about Jesus and feel your faith should play a more important role in your life but you aren't sure how to go about doing that. Or, even worse, you've tried to make your faith more important but every single thing you've tried has sputtered out and you aren't sure what to do next.

How do you get from knowing about Jesus to knowing Jesus Himself?

This book is not going to try to introduce you to who Jesus is. You already know who Jesus is. Maybe you've even met Him in a personal way. What you want to know now is what happens next. What happens once you already know about Jesus or have met Him for that first time? How do you go from that first meeting with God to a lasting, daily kind of relationship with Him?

Jesus didn't come and do all of the things He did so we would just know about Him. He isn't a celebrity trying to get His name out to as many people as possible so they will buy His stuff and support His career. We have an infinite God with plans for us which stretch across time and space. A celebrity-style mission is not big enough for God: He wants more.

Jesus came so that we would know Him and so that we could be with Him forever in Heaven. He wants us to be saints. So many times, though, we get caught up in the excitement of meeting Jesus and we want to stay there in the excitement of that first encounter. Meeting Jesus is important, yes, but God doesn't want us to stay in a place of meeting Him for the first time over and over again forever. He wants to have a relationship with us and He wants that relationship to start even before we get to Heaven.

In one of the letters in the New Testament, St Paul gets after the church at Corinth when he says this: *Do you not know that your body is a temple of the Holy Spirit within you, which you have from God? (1 Cor 6:19a)* That's not just a sassy line St Paul uses to make his lecture stick. We have a God who wants to be with us while we're still here on earth. He wants a personal, daily kind of relationship with us. It's in pursuing this kind of a relationship with God while we're here on earth that we prepare ourselves to be with Him in Heaven.

In this book, you'll find chapters which will help you in moving from knowing about Jesus to building a relationship with Him so you can know Him better. This isn't a concept book full of fancy words and theories. Each chapter is going to have things you can do right now to start building and deepening your relationship with God.

Don't worry—it's not super complicated! It's not going to be super complicated, but it will take some level of commitment from you just like it does when you build relationships with other people. There will be some effort and perseverance involved as you work on growing in your faith. This book will help you figure out where to direct your efforts next as you move from that first meeting with Jesus (knowing about Him) to having a daily kind of relationship with Him (knowing Him).

1 - WHO IS GOD TO YOU?

He said to them, "But who do you say that I am?"
(Mt 16:15)

Jesus asks His disciples this question one day while traveling around Judea. He starts out by asking them who other people say He is. Then He asks them the more pointed question: "Who do *you* say that I am?"

By this point in the Gospel narrative, the disciples have been walking around with Jesus for some time. They've seen Him teaching and working miracles, and they know a lot about Him from being with Him so much. But Jesus wasn't asking them a question about what He'd been doing. He didn't want them to recite back something He said in the temple last time He was teaching there. He didn't want them to pat Him on the back for the latest miracle He had worked. He was asking them about something else.

This question has more to do with relationship. Jesus wanted to know what kind of role the disciples thought He was going to play in their lives. Their answer wasn't going to change who Jesus actually was—He would still be God even if they thought He was just another prophet—but depending on their answer it would change the way they chose to relate to Him. If Jesus was just another man they wouldn't relate to Him the same way as they would if they believed He was God. The role He would play in their lives would be very different depending on who they saw Him as.

Notice how personal and direct this question is. When it comes to His relationship with His disciples what other people said didn't matter as much as what the disciples believed and said as individuals. The whole world could believe Jesus was God, but if the disciples didn't believe it than they weren't going to relate to Jesus as God. Who they each said He was mattered immensely for the type of relationship each one of them was going to be able to have with Him.

Jesus didn't just ask that question of his disciples 2000 years ago. He asks that same question of us today: Who do you say that I am?

Some people have a very distant view of God.

God is the creator who made everything. God is the king of the universe. God is a judge sitting in Heaven who watches His creatures down below. All of these ideas of who God is have an element of truth to them. They aren't the whole picture, though. Just like it wouldn't be fair to describe a priest as someone who just hears confessions we don't get the whole picture of who God is by looking at only one aspect of Him. If we want to get to know God fully than we have to expand our view of Him past just what He does to who He is.

There's a huge difference between knowing about God and knowing God. We get confused about this sometimes. We think that just knowing about God and doing what He says is enough. That we just have to acknowledge the instruction sheet we get and follow what's on it as closely as possible as if we were putting together a piece of IKEA furniture. God wants to be more than just known about, though. He wants to be known and to know us in return.

God isn't just an abstract idea. Jesus didn't relate to people as if He or they were abstract ideas. Jesus related to people in a personal, concrete way. The fact Jesus came and died on a cross to save us from our sins shows us that God is not a distant dictator. He doesn't only want to direct His creations around like little pawns in a board game without having real, personal involvement with them.

Our God doesn't want to stay at arm's length.

He wants involvement in the daily concerns of our lives. At one point Jesus is talking about the nation of Israel and He says: *How often would I have gathered your children together as a hen gathers her brood under her wings, and you would not! (Lk 13:34b)* God wants to be close to us. Jesus' lament in this verse is that He wanted to be close to the nation of Israel but they would not come close to Him.

The lament of Jesus in the Gospel of Luke brings us to another point. Did you ever think you could prevent God from getting something He wanted? Sometimes we think of God as someone who has (or can get) whatever He wants whenever He wants it. God didn't just create us because He thought it was a nice idea, though. He wants to relate personally to each and every one of us. We can prevent God from having that kind of relationship with us if we refuse to draw close to Him.

God is everywhere at every moment. There is nowhere we can go on this Earth that He isn't going to be there. When I say we can prevent God from being close to us, I mean we can shut Him out of our lives or force Him to stay at arm's length by the way we choose to relate to Him. Refusal of a close relationship with God is an option. He leaves the decision up to us.

You can think of it like when you were at school. There were people you passed in the hall every day who you might know by sight but who weren't in your friends circle. If one of them wanted to be your friend but you didn't want to be friends with them you could prevent them from getting to know you better by avoiding them or ignoring them when they approached. We can do the same thing with God. Even though He longs to be close to us we can prevent Him from being close to us by choosing not to get close to Him.

One of the ways we can prevent God from getting closer to us is by the choices we make. Every time we choose sin over God we are putting a wedge between ourselves and Him, pushing ourselves further away. Another way we can prevent God from having a close relationship with us is by the way we see God and who we say He is to us. How we picture His role in our life is going to influence the kind of relationship we're able to have with Him.

There are probably as many different ways of thinking about God as there are people walking around on Earth. Even though we can lump these different ways into categories there are still differences from person to person based on how mature their relationship with God is. Here are just a handful of different ways to view God and His role in our lives: Distant Creator, Stern Judge, Captain, Mentor or Coach, and Loving Father. Each one of these views leads to a different way of relating to God as we will see in the examples below.

Distant Creator

One of the things we know about God is that He made everything. The first two chapters of Genesis tell us God made everything out of nothing. Everything we have is a gift from God to us. While seeing God as the creator of everything is a good thing, seeing Him as a distant creator is an obstacle if we are wanting a closer relationship with Him. If this is our view of God than it isn't likely we would even think a close relationship with Him is possible.

A distant creator doesn't care very much about his creation after the work of creating it is over and done with. Maybe he admires it from afar every now and again, but he doesn't have daily involvement with it. He certainly isn't likely to care about the small details of what happens to it after he sets it in motion. This kind of a creator has no relationship with his work after the work of creating it is done. He sets it in motion and either steps back from it to watch or walks away from it entirely.

If this is our view of God than even if we wanted to have a close relationship with Him it wouldn't be possible. God wouldn't care about us anymore after creating us. No matter how hard we tried we wouldn't be able to get to know Him better because He'd be too distant and He wouldn't care about getting to know us better either.

If we lean towards seeing God as a distant creator than most likely we will believe and live as if God doesn't have much impact on our life now He has set it in motion.

We know from the Bible God isn't a distant creator. He told us so not only in Luke 13:34 where He talks about gathering Israel like a hen gathers her chicks but also in other places of the Bible. One of those places is that most famous verse: *For God so loved the world that he gave his only-begotten Son, that whoever believes in him should not perish but have eternal life. (Jn 3:16)* A God who gives His only son to save us after we drove the wedge of sin between Him and us is not a distant creator who no longer cares about His creation. He has not written us off to fend for ourselves or stepped away from us.

Our God wants to be involved with His creation.

Stern Judge

Some people believe God wants to be involved with His creation but that His involvement is like that of a stern judge who is only there to enforce the rules. A judge is someone who has authority. He decides whether I did something right or wrong and hands out punishment when I break the rules. Judges are also supposed to be impartial: they don't take sides or get personally involved with the people they are judging. Stern also implies inflexible. A stern judge doesn't allow exceptions for things which were out of my control. He cares about the rules and how well the rules have been followed but not about me or my unique situation.

While it is true God is the judge of this world we see time and time again in the Bible that He forgives sinners with an abundance of mercy. Whether it's the story of the woman caught in adultery (Jn 8:3-11) or Jesus' statement: *"Those who are well have no need of a physician, but those who are sick; I have not come to call the righteous, but sinners to repentance." (Lk 5:31b-32)* He shows His desire is to bring us closer to the Father. Jesus did not come to Earth as a spy from God to find out who was being naughty and didn't deserve entrance into Heaven. He came so we could have eternal life and not perish.

When we view God as a stern judge we're admitting He has some involvement with His creation but we're still viewing Him as distant and impersonal. This sort of view of God leads to a belief that while He does have an impact on my life it's probably going to be an unpleasant one. A stern judge is more likely to punish me for breaking the rules than to want to get to know me better.

If we see God this way we also aren't likely to want to get to know Him better either. If we think God is just watching and waiting for us to put a toe out of line so He can smite us back into our place than we aren't likely to want to get closer to Him. The closer we are to Him, the better He will see every time we mess something up.

God is our final judge, but He also wants us to

be with Him forever. He is looking for every opportunity to extend mercy to us and to invite us to be with Him. He knows we're going to fall, but He gives us many opportunities to get back up again and He isn't out looking to kick us while we're down. He isn't a stern judge who wants nothing more to do with us other than to decide whether something we did was right or wrong.

St Paul, when he was speaking to the men of Athens while bearing witness to Christ, says this about God:

> *The God who made the world and everything in it, being Lord of heaven and earth, does not live in shrines made by man, nor is he served by human hands, as though he needed anything, since he himself gives to all men life and breath and everything…Yet he is not far from each one of us… (Acts 17:24-25, 27b)*

St Paul is saying God does more than just make sure we follow the rules correctly. He doesn't just come to be worshiped and adored and get stuff from man whether it be obedience or material goods. God who is separate and apart from man, who needs nothing from man, gives everything to man down to his very life and being.

Our God wants more than just to be our judge.

Captain
Some people view God more as a military

leader. He is the one who has the vision for victory. He knows the best battle plan against our common enemy and He issues orders to us His troops so that His plan can be carried out. He maintains order and discipline. He cares about His people to the extent they stay fit and able to get the job done. He cares more about our competence for the mission than He does about us as individuals.

This view of God is somewhat similar to the Stern Judge when it comes to order and discipline. It's slightly different, however, in that a good captain is more involved with the well-being of his men as well as having a strong determination to make sure the mission is carried out properly.

It is true God has a plan and purpose for our lives: *For I know the plans I have for you, says the LORD, plans for welfare and not for evil, to give you a future and a hope. (Jer 29:11)* It is also true God is the one in charge. He gives us important guidelines for how to carry out our individual missions through the commandments and teachings of the Church He founded. God is someone who should be respected and obeyed, just like a commanding officer on the battlefield.

While it's good to see God as ultimately in charge, seeing Him as a captain or a military leader tends to limit his involvement in our life down to just making sure the mission He gives us is carried out. A military-style mission tends to have a specific focus and not carry over into every single aspect of our lives. It also tends to have more emphasis placed on making sure the mission is accomplished than on the individual men and women who are working to carry it out.

God wants more for us then just making sure the mission He has for us gets carried out properly. He wants to be with us. Another way of saying this would be that God ultimately cares more for us than He cares about the plan that He has for us. He cares about the plan, yes, but He cares more about us than about what we can do for Him.

It's really easy to get fixated on doing things for God and forget that, much as God appreciates it when we respond to His invitations to do things for Him, what He really wants is to be with us. We see this in the Gospel story of Martha and Mary (Lk 10:38-42). Jesus went to visit with these two sisters one day. Martha was running around serving people while Mary sat at the feet of Jesus and listened to what He had to say. Martha complained to Jesus, telling Him to tell her sister to get up and help her. Jesus' response to Martha was that Mary, who was sitting at His feet, had chosen the better part. Jesus cared about being with them more than about what they could do for Him in that moment.

A captain who is concerned with running a tight ship cares about how well things are running and how his men can help him accomplish the mission. God cares about us to an extent which goes beyond just making sure the mission is handled efficiently.

Mentor or Coach

Some people believe God does want to be involved with His creation. They see His role in their lives as being more of a mentor or a divine life coach. God is that person who is wiser that they can turn to when they need help with something which is too big for them to handle on their own.

Coaches and mentors are great when it comes to handling specific problems. Whether it's learning how to get better at sports or needing help to figure out what to major in at college or what type of work to pursue, you're lucky if you had a good coach or mentor who could give you some solid advice and help you out. Although they didn't swoop in and magically make all your problems and issues disappear they were there to give you advice and strategies. Coaches and mentors are good at helping you improve in your weak spots, work on overcoming your problems, and put your best foot forward so you can grow into a better person.

Coaches and mentors tend to be more involved with our personal lives then either a distant creator or a stern judge would be. Their involvement is usually limited to one area of our life, however. They are the sports coach or the career mentor. The advice they give and the help they offer tend to be more focused on helping you with that one problem area of your life, not your whole life. They may be happy when the rest of your life is going well and some of what they say may help you with the other areas of your life too but your conversations tend to focus on the one or two issues you want help with.

When we view God as more of a coach or mentor we tend to only come to Him when we have specific problems we want Him to fix in certain areas of our life. We are trusting He cares enough about us to fix it but we're also only coming to Him with those specific problems we want Him to solve. God isn't allowed into the other areas of our life we don't want to bring up. He's like the specialist doctor for my foot that I won't ever talk about my kidneys or sinuses with.

While the coach or mentor view does allow for a closer relationship with God, it still limits His involvement to only certain areas or things. God becomes someone I only go to when I need help or advice even if it is a regularly scheduled meeting to get that help or advice.

Seeing God this way means I box up parts of my life and I only let Him see certain things. He doesn't get access to all of my life. I'm not going to bring Him the parts of my life where everything is going well (because I don't need Him to fix them for me) and I'm also only going to want to talk to Him about the certain things I want Him to solve for me. Other areas in my life are off limits to Him.

God doesn't want to be limited in His

relationship with us. He wants full and total access to our lives and to be with us in every moment from the best to the worst. If we have a coach or a mentor view of God's role, we are naturally going to limit Him to only those places where we think we need Him.

God wants more than just to be there to help us with our problems.

Loving Father

The idea of God as a loving father is hard for most of us to embrace. We have all kinds of associations with the word "Father" which are based on how our fathers treated us. Nobody has a perfect earthly father who can be used as a perfect model to describe how God would fill this kind of role in our life.

This view of God as a loving father, while harder for us to get our minds around, is closer to understanding the kind of role God does want to play in our lives. Jesus says we are to address God as "Father" when He teaches us the Lord's prayer (Mt 6:9-13). Except that our translation of the word into English is a little off. Almost every Bible translates it into English using the word "Father" when scholars tell us a better translation would be "Daddy." There's a world of different meanings attached to the words "Father" and "Daddy." "Father" tends to be understood as formal and somewhat distant. The word "Daddy", on the other hand, usually invokes for people a closer, more loving relationship than "Father" does.

A loving father is not just someone you go to when you have a problem you need help with. He's not just someone you check in with at the end of the day to say what you did right and wrong in order to get your deserved reward or punishment. A loving father, a daddy, wants to be involved in every single detail of your life.

Loving fathers aren't scared away by the messiness or difficulty of their children's lives. They are committed 100% and more to the good of their children. This is a level of commitment to the child's good which reaches even beyond the level of commitment to his own good that the child has sometimes. It is a level of commitment and love which wants good for the child even when the child would rather not have that good. This is the kind of relationship God wants with us: to love us totally and completely in every moment of our lives. Nothing is too big or too small for Him to be concerned with when it comes to us.

This is the kind of view of God Jesus and His mother Mary had. They understood God wanted to be involved in every moment of their lives. No part of their life was off limits to God. They knew they could come to God with everything in an attitude of trustful surrender because they knew that – even if it was uncomfortable or an answer they didn't like—God was going to handle it in the way that was truly best for them.

We see this view of God in the 'Fiat' Mary gives

at the Annunciation (Lk 1:38) when the angel Gabriel tells her she is to be the mother of God. Contained in her 'Fiat' is an immense trust everything was going to be alright. She knew God was going to be there even when the way became difficult. We see this view of God again in the 'Fiat' Jesus gives to the Father in Gethsemane as He is on the threshold of beginning His passion and death. He trusted the Father enough to know that even though the present way was difficult it was going to be handled in the way that was best.

This kind of trust is something which grows as our faith in God grows. Our ability to trust in God as Mary and Jesus did will increase as we get closer to Him. St Paul speaks about this in the letter to the Romans when he says: *We know that in everything God works for good with those who love him, who are called according to his purpose. (Rom 8:28)*

This kind of relationship, one which trusts God in each and every circumstance of life, is one which God wants with each and every one of us. The only ones who were able to live it fully here on Earth were Jesus and Mary. Each and every one of the saints, however, tried to live out this kind of relationship with God, and it is a relationship He continually invites us to.

The above are some broad categories of how we can see our relationship with God. Depending on which of these categories I tend to put God into,

I'm going to have a different set of ideas of how to relate to God and what kind of a role He's going to play in my life. Each one of these ways of viewing God leads to a relationship which has a different level of closeness and trust in God. We can even say every single one of them has a different level of potential intimacy in the relationship.

Intimacy gets a twisted kind of meaning today. The original meaning of the word is similar to a depth measurement: how open and vulnerable we are being with someone when we share our lives with them. Another way of thinking of it is how well do we know them and how well do we let them know us.

When it comes to having intimacy with God that's exactly what we mean: how well do we know God and how well do we let Him know us. Our idea of who God is—how we see Him and His role in our life—can hinder our ability to build a close, intimate relationship with Him. In fact, how we see God will drive the kind of relationship we build with Him.

God wants a deeply intimate relationship with us. He doesn't want to be a God kept at arm's length. Remember the words of Jesus we read at the beginning of the chapter: *How often would I have gathered your children together as a hen gathers her brood under her wings, and you would not! (Lk 13:34b)* God wants to truly love us, not just a love that consists of warm, fuzzy feelings when He thinks about us. God's love took the Son to the arms of the cross so that we would be saved.

God is inviting us to be saints, to be people who are with Him forever in Heaven. If we accept this invitation that means we're going to be spending a lot of time with God. Would you want to spend forever with someone you had no relationship with? Part of the good news is that we don't have to wait until we get to heaven to start working on this relationship. We can start now. We can begin transforming into the type of people who want to be with God forever in heaven as saints.

If you've ever dated someone, or even just watched the relationships of your friends who are dating, you know that good relationships don't just "sort of happen" by accident. They take work and attention. The same thing is true of our relationship with God. A good relationship with God does not happen by accident. We have to put attention and some effort into our relationship with God if we want it to grow just as we have to with the other relationships in our lives. The good news is God does most of the work in our relationship with Him. We do have to be willing to take a step towards Him, though. Taking that step means we need to be intentional in our pursuit of a better relationship with God. It isn't something that "just happens" if we don't put any attention or effort into it.

In order to pursue a closer relationship with God, we have to leave behind a checklist or contract mentality when it comes to religion. We can't view relationship building as something we are making progress in if we just accomplish a certain list of tasks. We need to remember heaven isn't something earned by checking off all of the right boxes. We need to transform our contract mentality of relationship with God into a covenant mentality.

Contracts are legal documents which say if I do X, Y, and Z you will give me something specific in return. Covenants are different. Covenants are exchanges of persons. There is no checklist of accomplishments we must have in order to get into heaven like a list of admission requirements at college or university. We don't earn our way into heaven by fulfilling all of the requirements of the contract because there is no contract. Our relationship with God is a covenant. We tend to try to bring in a contract mentality when it comes to dealing with God because it's less effort.

God wants a relationship with us. He tells us to come to Him like little children (Mt 18:2-3). Children don't have a filter. They think everything is important. They say exactly what is on their mind without worrying what other people will think. This is how God is asking us to come to Him: with no filter and with total trust.

Good relationships don't just happen, though, they take work. Part of being a committed follower of Jesus is learning how to build a good relationship with Him. One of the most important things we can do to build a good relationship (whether it's with God or someone else) is to learn how to communicate with them. We communicate with God through prayer. In the next few chapters, we're going to talk about prayer and how to approach it in a way which helps us pursue a deeper relationship with God.

Ask Yourself:

1.) Who do I say that God is?

2.) Of the five categories of relationship discussed in the chapter (distant creator, stern judge, captain, coach or mentor, loving father) which one seems closest to how I relate to God?

3.) Do I want to improve my relationship with God or am I good with it the way it is?

Take Action:

1.) Pick a word which describes your relationship with God. Write it down. Address it to Him, i.e. "God you are...to me."

2 - GETTING TO KNOW YOU

"God loves each of us as if there were only one of us." – St Augustine

Do you have the same relationship with your best friend today as you did that very first day you met them?

Unless you met your best friend yesterday the answer is probably "No." Relationships change as we go through different experiences (together or apart) and get to know each other better. Unless you are growing apart this kind of change is good for the relationship. Would you want your relationship with your best friend to be the same today as it was that first day you met them? If it was, you probably wouldn't be best friends. You would always be in a stage of "Nice to meet you!"

Good relationships take time and effort. They aren't something that just happens overnight. We don't have the same kind of relationship with someone we've just met as we do with our best friend. As we put time and effort into getting to know the other person our relationship with them changes. It's still important that you met them that first time because otherwise there wouldn't even be a relationship. That first meeting isn't as important, though, to the kind of relationship you have today as everything which has happened since then.

The same thing is true when it comes to our relationship with God. It's important that we meet God, but if we want to develop a good relationship with Him then what happens after we've met Him is more important than that first meeting.

God really wants to be close to us and to get to know us better. Sometimes we think that God just gets (or takes) whatever He wants because He's God. When it comes to a relationship with us, God doesn't just snap His fingers and then automatically we're best friends. He doesn't come charging in after our first meeting with Him and immediately take up residence as the most important person in our life.

That's because God doesn't force Himself on us. The Catechism of the Catholic Church (CCC)[1] tells

---

[1] The CCC is a compilation of the Catholic Church's teachings

us that "God willed that man should be 'left in the hand of his own counsel,' so that he might of his own accord seek his Creator and freely attain his full and blessed perfection by cleaving to him." (CCC 1730). In the first chapter, we heard the lament of Jesus: *How often would I have gathered your children together as a hen gathers her brood under her wings, and you would not! (Lk 13:34b)* God desires for us to be close to Him, but He does not force Himself on us. He leaves it up to our choice.

If we want a closer relationship with God He is ready and waiting for us. He is ready to be close to us and waiting on our free choice in the matter. If we want to be closer to God than we have to put some time and effort into building our relationship with Him. Remember, good relationships don't "just happen" by accident.

When it comes to building relationships there are two things which are pretty key in going from just met to best friends. First, there has to be a desire to know the other person better. If you don't have that desire, why would you even put forth the effort? Second, there should be some kind of regular contact with that person.

Normally we have to see someone a few times before we start thinking about them as a friend. One thing we usually do as the friendship grows is to take that person out of their usual setting (where we normally hang out at school or work)

---

on faith and morals.

and bring them into different settings with us: the movies, a restaurant, etc. This is because we don't just want to see them in one place; we're happy to see them and be with them everywhere. The last thing we would try to do is to make it so that we are forever "just meeting" them. We want each meeting following the first one to build a relationship which is something more than "we just met."

God doesn't want to keep encountering us in a just-met kind of way over and over again. He wants to get to know us as we really are and to be in an eternal relationship with us. If we're going to get past the "Hi, nice to meet you," stage of our relationship with God that means we're going to have to put some effort into spending time with Him.

One of the best ways to get to know someone is by talking to them. When we spend time talking to God in prayer we get to know Him better and He gets to know us better. In order to grow our relationship with God, we need to get to where we see prayer as sharing time with God and not just punching a clock. If we're just punching the clock than we're not actually serious about wanting to get to know God better.

If we approach talking to God as just saying a bunch of words and we don't put our person and attention behind the words we say than we're missing out on building a real, lasting relationship with Him. If our prayer time is just one more thing on our to-do list that we have to finish if we want to stay out of hell than we are missing the point of what prayer actually is. We're also missing out on a relationship which is worth having just because we wouldn't give it the time and effort it needed to grow.

One of the things the Catechism says about prayer is this: "…prayer is the encounter of God's thirst with ours. God thirsts that we may thirst for him." (CCC 2560). That's great, but what does that mean?

When was the last time you were really thirsty? Maybe you were out walking on a hot day or eating salty French Fries and you just had to have a drink of something right *now*. Can you feel the longing in that kind of thirst? Any kind of liquid, no matter what, will do as long as it eases that awful thirst. That's the kind of thirst God has for us. He is thirsty for our presence and attention.

We too are thirsty for God even though we don't always realize it. The restless dissatisfaction with life and longing for more which we feel from time to time is actually a thirst for God. Sometimes we've been thirsty for so long we just kind of try to ignore it because we aren't dying from it and we aren't sure how to get rid of it. Ignoring it doesn't make it go away, though. That thirst still needs to be quenched with something and the sooner the better.

What the Catechism is saying is when we pray (i.e. talk to God) it's like our longing for Him is meeting His longing for us. The more time we spend with God and the more we realize the thirst He has to pour out His love on us the thirstier we will get for Him. When we come to God in prayer, when we spend time with Him, both we and He have our thirst for each other's presence satisfied. It's like when you haven't seen your best friend for weeks and you're missing them and they're missing you and you finally see each other again. That meeting satisfies the longing you both had to see each other.

The Catechism goes on to say: "Thus, the life of prayer is the habit of being in the presence of the thrice-holy God and in communion with him." (CCC 2565) To get to know God better, to be "in communion with him", we need to make prayer a habit. Not a habit as in something I have to do, like brush my teeth. A habit as in something we make time for because we want to do it, like eating. And just like eating, prayer is something we thrive on when we do it every single day.

How well do you think you can get to know someone if you hardly ever spend time with them? Or what if you don't talk to them very often? You're going to be spending so much time catching up on events you don't have much time to learn more about who they are. We need to make time for God so regularly that it becomes a habit for us just like checking both ways before we step across the street is.

We need to make prayer and spending time with

God a priority in our lives.

To help us do this we may need to change the way we think about prayer. Prayer is not just saying a bunch of words which go into this void place where maybe God hears it and maybe He doesn't. It isn't like typing an email or a text message where we can start, stop, go back, re-edit, or do it with our mind on something else and the other person doesn't notice because they only get the finished message at the end.

Prayer is a conversation, not texting. If someone was trying to talk to you, thirsting to get to know you better, and you were sitting across from them looking at someone else, letting your sentences drop half-finished from your lips, or constantly looking at your phone to see who else was trying to talk to you how important are they going to think they are to you?

The truth is, despite what we may try to tell ourselves, prayer is not just saying words. Even if they are the right words, we aren't having a conversation if our heart and attention aren't behind the words when we say them. Prayer is more than just words: it's an attitude. It's a movement of our heart towards God. We are not actually praying if we approach prayer with a checklist mentality, as just one more thing we have to do, which we rush through in order to move on to something else.

The Catechism makes this clear: "According to Scripture, it is the *heart* that prays. If our heart is

far from God, the words of prayer are in vain."
(CCC 2562). This is even mentioned in scripture.
Jesus quotes the prophet Isaiah saying: *'This people honors me with their lips, but their heart is far from me; in vain do they worship me, teaching as doctrines the precepts of men.' (Mt 15:8-9)*

The truth is, even if you feel like you've just met Christ and don't really know Him that well, your relationship with God is the most important relationship in your life. It is well worth the time and effort it takes on your part to build a good relationship with Him.

Prayer is not about checking off all the boxes to be able to say we have prayed and met our duty. It's about building a relationship with God. The disciplines of certain forms of prayer are there to help us prepare for an encounter with God and to make it easier for us to build a relationship with Him. The disciplines are not the end all be all, though, when it comes to communion with God. We can't let ourselves get so focused on whether we are doing everything exactly right that we forget to actually pay attention to God during our prayer time.

We need to ask ourselves this question: what kind of relationship am I building with God? If I say God is important in my life, do my actions show that? Am I acting as if God were the most important person in my life? Or am I even acting as if He is a person who I do want in my life?

The way we talk to people is going to determine

the kind of relationship we can have with them. Over the next couple of pages, we're going to look at some things we might need to address in our current attitude towards prayer if we want to go deeper in our relationship with God.

Prayer is about building intimacy

We talked about what intimacy was (a measure of how much sharing happens in a relationship) in the previous chapter when we talked about how we see God. Another way you can think of intimacy is as meaning "into-me-see": the more vulnerable and open you are with people, the more intimacy you have with them. The more you know about someone and the more they know about you the more intimate you are with each other. If you barely know someone than you don't know very much about them and they don't know very much about you. If you have an intimate relationship with someone than they know a lot about you and you know a lot about them. We can think about intimacy as a sliding scale where we can take steps towards knowing someone better and better from the time we first meet them.

This is another awesome thing about God: He's a gentleman and doesn't force Himself on us. He gave us free will and that means we can freely choose how we are going to respond to His invitation to know Him better. We talked above about how God thirsts for us. He thirsts for us, but He also knocks politely instead of kicking down the door of our heart demanding to be let in. You can keep God out of your life. He won't go peeking behind doors you have shut in His face.

Part of getting to know God better is getting to the point where you trust Him enough to let Him behind those doors you don't let just anyone behind. This means as we get more intimate with God we're going to be praying about different things going on in our life. We wouldn't tell a stranger all of the details of a big fight we just had with someone else who really hurt our feelings by what they said. If God is closer to us than our best friend, this is exactly the kind of thing He wants to hear about from us.

Every time we pray is a chance to grow closer to God by sharing more of what's going on in our life with Him. This includes even the bad stuff we don't really want to talk about with anyone and would rather hide.

Quality is more important than quantity

Quality is more important than quantity but remember you must have some quantity of prayer in order for there to be a relationship!

We see the quality over quantity issue play out in our day to day life. Think about someone important to you. Do you go and say "Hi!" to them every day? Maybe not. Do you give them your full attention when you're with them? You try to if you value the relationship. Same thing with God. Do you value your relationship with

Him enough to spend quality time with Him? Or are you trying to get fire insurance by meeting the minimum policy requirements?

Let's say you go to the coffee shop every day. Every day the same person is behind the counter waiting to take your order. If you meet this person every day and say the exact same things but nothing else, how deep is your relationship with that person? Not very. I mean, they probably have your coffee order down if you get the same thing every time, but that's about it. You don't know them and they don't know you.

Now let's say you visit your cousin once a month for an hour. While you're with your cousin you share things going on in your life and he shares things going on in his life. You don't see that cousin as often as you do the person behind the counter in the coffee shop. You may not even spend the same quantity of time with that cousin but the quality of the time spent together is higher. You are sharing your life with your cousin on a more meaningful level. This means the relationship you have with your cousin is deeper, more intimate, than the relationship you have with the person behind the counter in the coffee shop.

The quantity of time we spend in prayer is not as important as the depth of the sharing that occurs—although do keep in mind that quantity is still important.

Prayer is in part recognizing the presence of God

and responding to it. God is always present to us, but we aren't always present to Him. When we focus on quality instead of quantity, we are making an effort to be present to Him in a meaningful way. It's just like when you are having dinner with friends or family and you all put your phones down to concentrate on each other for that space of time. The quality of the time spent together goes up the more of our attention and presence we put into it.

Attention is more important than activity

There are many types of prayer, just as there are many types of ways of spending time with people you love.

When it comes to daily prayer, it is more important that our attention is fixed on God than that we specifically say a certain number or type of prayers. We can't just read the Bible or sing praise and worship songs with our mind on something else and truly say we are praying. If we do, we fall into the problem of praying with our lips while our heart is far from God which the prophet Isaiah warned us about.

If you think you are praying just because you read your Bible without your full attention on the words you are reading than you are using a checklist mentality instead of a relationship mentality when you approach prayer. How we pray is important. We have to put our heart (not just our lips) into what we are doing.

Sometimes we think that just because we are doing something, and it is getting done, we are doing an okay job. This might work with sweeping the floor or folding clothes but it doesn't work when you are trying to build a good, lasting relationship. You have to put your attention and heart behind what you are doing.

There are a lot of different activities when it comes to prayer. Some people go to Mass during the week, say a rosary, visit Jesus in the Eucharist, meditate on scripture, sing praise and worship songs—there are so many different ways to pray it can get overwhelming. It's also impossible to do every single one of these activities every single day. This shouldn't discourage us or leave us wanting to just blow off prayer altogether though just because it's impossible to do all of the good things every single time.

Imagine for a second you are dating someone trying to discern marriage. You don't always go to the coffee shop when you go on a date. You don't always talk about the exact same things. In fact, what you do may not matter to you so much as that you are doing something together and it's serving as a method of getting to know each other better. The same thing can happen in your relationship with God. What you do is not as important for building a relationship as that your attention and heart are present to the other person in what you are doing.

There is one exception to this. The church, as our

mother, does require that we pray in certain ways at certain times. We must go to Mass on Sunday and Holy Days of Obligation (CCC 2042). The Code of Canon Law[2] does allow exceptions for grave reasons (Canon 1248). Normally those grave reasons are things like illness, the need to travel or to work to support your family, or the lack of a priest to celebrate Mass.

The precept about Mass attendance is in place because the Church teaches if we didn't follow this without a grave reason not to than we would be causing a terrible wound to our relationship with God. In fact, one of the things the Catechism tells us to emphasize the importance of the Mass is that "…the Church has always venerated the Scriptures as she venerates the Lord's Body. She never ceases to present to the faithful the bread of life, taken from the one table of God's Word and Christ's Body." (CCC 103) That table is presented to us at each and every Mass. Our presence at Mass is extremely important to us and to our relationship with God. When I say that what we do isn't as important as that our attention is behind it I don't mean you should ignore the precepts of the Church.

Another thing I am not saying is that particular devotions which involve you saying certain prayers are bad or not important. These things

---

[2] The Code of Canon Law is a compilation of the Church's laws. It is ecclesiastical as opposed to governmental law.

have their place. We need to recognize that devotions are only helpful in so far as they help us to grow closer to God. They are not an end in and of themselves. So if you feel terrible because you've never been able to get into a particular devotion everyone else seems to be raving about: relax. God likes variety. There are many different ways to pray and they are all worth pursuing as long as they help you to get closer to God.

Relationships take time to build

Communication is important in every relationship, but we don't just meet someone and start dishing out our whole life story to them. There has to be a process where we share more of ourselves as we get more comfortable with and learn to trust each other. The same thing happens with God. Most of us don't just immediately trust God with every part of our lives all at once. As we grow in prayer, we work on trusting God enough to open up to Him those parts of our life that we normally don't talk about with people we've just met.

This is one of the places where daily communication becomes more important. The deeper your relationship with God gets, the more of yourself (both the good and the bad) you will want to share with Him. Even if it's only a few minutes a day, a daily conversation with God helps us to build that trust and familiarity with Him which will deepen the intimacy of our relationship with Him.

You may find yourself drawn to certain ways of praying as you start to spend more time in prayer, and that's okay. Your prayer life should be changing and getting deeper as you grow closer to God. Just because you've been using one method of prayer for a while doesn't mean you need to hang onto it for your whole life. It's okay to try different methods even if it means you have to put others aside for a while.

The end goal is not perfect devotion to one method of prayer but devotion to getting closer to God. If we insist on hanging onto something even when it isn't working, we run the risk of beginning to worship the method of prayer instead of the one we are praying to.

Now that we've talked about some of the attitudes behind our prayer we're going to talk more about the actions of prayer and how to figure out which actions to use.

Ask Yourself:

1.) How well do I know God?

2.) How well do I let God know me?

3.) Do I want to let God get to know me better?

Take Action:

1.) List the types of prayer you have tried before. What did you like or not like about them?

2.) Take God out of His normal setting. Try saying a type of prayer you normally wouldn't.

3 - WHAT DO I SAY?

Likewise the Spirit helps us in our weakness; for we do not know how to pray as we ought, but the Spirit himself intercedes for us with sighs too deep for words. (Rom 8:26)

Have you ever tried to start praying and then gotten overwhelmed?

There are so many different ways to pray: which one are you supposed to do? You can't possibly do everything every day. And what if you already do pray every day but want to deepen your prayer life? How do you even do that?

This chapter isn't going to introduce you to a bunch of different prayer methods. There are plenty of places where you can find that information. Instead, we're going to talk about general tips for prayer whether you're just starting out or looking to go deeper. Some prayer methods will be mentioned, but don't get worried if you don't know what they are or how to use them yet. The methods aren't as important as the attitude we put behind them.

One of the worst things you can do in a relationship is to make talking to the other person something that you're just checking off of a to-do list. Talking to them shouldn't be something you're just trying to get out of the way so you can get on with more important stuff. Talking to them should be important to you. The same thing with prayer: if we take a checklist mentality into our conversation with God than we risk praying with our lips instead of with our hearts.

The first thing you want to make sure of is that you're praying consistently every day. We need regular contact with God if we want to get to know Him better and to let Him get to know us better. Whether you've never prayed before or have tried and failed more times than you care to admit, the following tips can help you get started with building and maintaining the habit of prayer.

Start small

Let's say you want to become a bodybuilder. You know you need to go to the gym and lift weights because that's what bodybuilders do. So you head to the gym and look around. All these other people are there and they're lifting 100 lbs weights. Not wanting to look like a fool or waste your time, you decide to start lifting 100 lbs weights. Maybe you manage to make it through your first workout doing that. You go home exhausted but pretty pleased with yourself for all the progress you made on your first day.

But what happens the next day when you wake up? Every single muscle you forced to lift those 100 lbs you weren't used to lifting is screaming at you. You're in so much pain you can barely get of bed. Not only that, you're still sore the next day and the day after that. Do you make it back to the gym to lift 100 lbs again that week? Not even! You can barely move. In fact, you may never go back to the gym at all if you now believe your goal was too hard and you just can't do it.

What went wrong?

You tried to do too much too soon. In your excitement over your new project, you tried to go from doing nothing to doing what the experienced weight lifters were doing all on the first day. You didn't take into account that this was not their first day at the gym, and then you got discouraged because you couldn't do what everyone else was doing right away.

We do this sort of thing a lot, especially when we're excited about a new resolution we've made. That's why the gyms are so crowded the first few weeks of January every year and then return to normal by February and March.

The same kind of thing can happen in our prayer life too.

We decide we want to build a prayer life and we look around to see what everyone else who has a prayer life is doing. Then we try to copy them or do everything they say we should be doing without taking into account where we're starting from. If we aren't used to prayer — whether praying that much or in that way — we can quickly burn out and get discouraged if we go all in all at once on the daily routine of someone who has made prayer a habit for years.

The trick to building a consistent prayer habit is simply this: start small.

But wait! Aren't we supposed to get as holy as we can as soon as we can? Why would you start with a baby step when you can take a bunch of big steps right away and get further along?

Let's return to our body builder example. You go to the gym with a goal in mind — become a great bodybuilder — but you've never lifted anything heavier than a suitcase before. You go over to the weight rack. There's a tiny set of dumbbells at the end (probably pink) which weighs 3 lbs. You know that isn't very heavy, and they feel ridiculously light when you pick them up, but you know it's better to start small because you want to build the habits which lead to becoming a bodybuilder. Since you are focused on building a habit, you complete a workout with the little pink weights.

The next day you wake up and are surprised to find you're a little sore. It hurts to move your arms and legs, and you know it's from lifting those ridiculously light weights the day before. You can still move around, though, and you go back to the gym and pick up the pink weights again. You hit the gym every day for two weeks learning the habit and learning the methods you need to build a strong foundation. Then one day you put the pink weights down and pick up the heavier set next to them. Then a few weeks later you go up again. Then you do it again. And again. Months down the road you're lifting those 100 lbs you were tempted to start with.

What happened? Small actions, done consistently, can lead to growth.

Big actions done once and never done again don't move us forward when it comes to building habits. When it comes to getting to know someone better, a daily phone call to check in for a few minutes is better than calling once a month to talk for an hour. You have to make a habit of calling for a few minutes a day before talking for half an hour every day doesn't seem like an awful burden or an imposition.

Start praying for a few minutes every day. Maybe it's five minutes. Maybe it's one Our Father and one Hail Mary. Whatever it is, be consistent and stick with it for a little while. Once you can do that ask yourself if you're ready to spend a few more minutes in prayer every day. Try to build up to ten or fifteen minutes a day. If you do that, you are well on your way to forming a consistent habit of daily prayer.

Don't pick something you don't like

This seems really obvious but we often mess up here too.

There are lots of different ways to pray. Which one are you supposed to do? Whether you're just starting out or trying to go deeper it's important not to pick something you don't like. If you pick something you don't like you aren't going to want to stay with it long enough for it to actually help you deepen your relationship with God.

We can easily fall into the trap of making prayer harder than it has to be. If you're trying to learn how to pray you probably asked for help or looked up ways that different people pray. If you did, you probably stumbled on some rule or discipline of prayer which holy people do. In Catholic circles that list probably looked something like this: daily Mass, daily Rosary, read your Bible, and make a Holy Hour in front of the Eucharist.

Maybe you decided to start small. Maybe you realized some things, like a daily Mass or Holy Hour, weren't going to be an option for you. So you said something like this to yourself: okay, I will say the Rosary every day and that will help me get closer to God. You started learning how to say the Rosary. And it was terrible. You were bad at it, your mind kept wandering, you got bored doing the same meditations every few days, and you really started to dread your prayer time because it was so difficult and it felt like you weren't getting anything out of it.

Maybe you are terrible at saying the Rosary. Maybe you just need to keep trying to say the Rosary until you get better at it. Or, maybe, the Rosary isn't a devotion which is going to help you at this point. There are lots of different ways to pray because we're all different. Some of us can sit still for hours and some of us can't and that's okay. The prayer method isn't as important as that whatever you do is helping you to get closer to God. If you find that praying a particular way is like pulling teeth and you flinch inside every time you think about it than find something else to try for your daily prayer time.

It's okay to stop praying in a certain way even if everyone else around you is raving about how helpful it is for them. Just don't use the fact you didn't like a certain way of praying as an excuse to stop praying altogether.

We're sometimes tempted to try to be a super-powered Christian and rush right into a new way or time of praying. Or worse, we start thinking that because it's difficult to pray a certain way we're building super awesome spiritual skills by gritting our teeth and powering through. We think that somehow this is working to make us even holier than we'd get if we did something easier.

You're actually just increasing the likelihood you're going to quit at this point. When you're trying to build a new habit you want to make it as easy for yourself as possible. Once you get the habit down you can start thinking about trying ways of prayer which are harder for you.

Have you tried the Rosary and found it wasn't for you? Try doing the daily Mass readings or one of the hours from Liturgy of the Hours. These aren't as repetitive as the Rosary. Are you trying to read your Bible but getting bogged down in the historical or prophetic books? Jump to the Gospels. Try to put yourself in the scene you're reading as one of the characters and see what you notice.

When you're trying a new prayer method, make sure you give it a decent shot before calling it quits. You tried something for two days and found it difficult? It's probably still too new for you to use it fluently. You tried something consistently for a month and you just hate it? It's probably time to make some adjustments. You know what that breaking point is where you've genuinely tried something and it just isn't working. Work with yourself, not against yourself. We do have to put time and effort into talking to God but it shouldn't be unbearably painful.

Also, keep in mind that some ways of praying need more time than others. As you get comfortable with spending more time in prayer you can begin using prayer methods which take longer. If you're trying to spend five minutes praying daily, don't pick something which needs ten minutes and then try to rush through it in five. It's better to pick something which either fits the amount of time you have or to realize you're going to need to work at spending more time in prayer if you want to use a method which takes longer.

Don't beat yourself up

It's so easy to make grand plans for how your prayer time is going to go, isn't it? It'll be peaceful, distraction-free, and you'll have a great time getting to know God better and pouring out your heart to Him.

Then life happens.

Or maybe you're imagining how much holier you'll be soon because of praying this new way. Then two weeks later you're stuck and hating it because you can't get yourself to do it. Or you keep trying but find you're terrible at it. Now what are you supposed to do?

Don't beat yourself up about it.

We often give up because we get discouraged when we find out something is harder than we thought or is taking longer than we think it should. If you're trying your best but things don't seem to be going your way there are a few things you can look at which might help make it easier to keep going.

Maybe you're praying at the wrong time of day.

Are you a night owl and trying to get up earlier to pray? That might be your problem. Especially when you're starting out, try not to pray at times when it's going to be difficult for you to keep your attention fixed on praying.

Maybe you're not in the right place. If you are someone who likes to focus and you're trying to pray while driving or in a noisy place that might be another reason you're having trouble. Try to find some place quieter.

Maybe you picked a prayer method which was a bit too hard for you right now. Try a different way of praying. Remember: the method you use for daily prayer is not as important as that it draws you closer to God.

Maybe you need some extra support in the form of a prayer buddy. You don't have to pray together, although that might help too. A prayer buddy can help you the same way an exercise partner or a study buddy does: they help keep you accountable for your goal by either praying with you or checking in with you to make sure you did pray when you said you were going to.

If you find you are getting distracted while praying, keep in mind that it's pretty much impossible to pray without any distractions. The trick is not to let your distractions control your prayer time. Just keep returning your heart and mind to God. It gets easier with practice but distractions never go away entirely.

Just like with any skill, it takes practice to get the

habits and methods of praying down smoothly. The more fluent you become in a way of prayer the easier it will be for you to keep your heart and mind focused on God.

Don't let discouragement keep you from praying. If you are getting discouraged because something isn't working, allow yourself a few seconds to feel sorry for yourself—don't try to pretend you aren't discouraged because that can make it worse—but then get back at it again. Ask if and where you need to make adjustments to keep going and then do it.

Maybe you have your daily prayer habit down and you're interested in learning how to pray more deeply. What are you supposed to do then?

When you're first building a prayer habit the type of prayer you do isn't as important as that you build the habit. Once you get the habit down to where you're praying regularly for ten to fifteen minutes at a time, though, it becomes more important to start thinking about how you're praying. Some types of prayer are going to make it easier for you to get to know God better and to share more of yourself with Him.

Again we run up against the issue of there being so many different ways to pray we can't possibly do them all in the same day. Which one is best? Or better yet, which one is best for you right now?

Here are a few things to keep in mind when you are starting to look for ways to deepen your prayer life once you have the habit down.

Transition from vocal to mental prayer

What's the difference between vocal and mental prayer?

Vocal prayer usually involves words which can be said out loud. It can be something like reciting an Our Father or something which combines different prayers together like the Liturgy of the Hours. Vocal prayers usually have a very set structure (like in the Mass) but they can also be spontaneous (praise, discussing your day with God, asking for help with a specific problem, etc.). Vocal prayers tend to be easier for us, and they are where you should start if you are new to prayer or trying to build up a consistent prayer habit.

Mental prayer is a little different and tends to be more difficult than vocal prayer. It generally falls into one of two categories: meditation or contemplation.

When I said 'meditation' your mind probably went to the wrong place. There's Eastern meditation and there's Christian meditation. Don't do Eastern meditation; do Christian meditation. What's the difference? In Eastern meditation the goal is to empty the self. It's more about union with the universe through losing sight of yourself. In Christian meditation the goal is to fill the self with more of God. It's about learning more about God so you can be the person God invites and desires you to be.

When we pray with the methods of meditation it usually involves really thinking through something and then talking to God about how it applies to our life. Usually, the something used is spiritual reading from either the Bible or one of the saints. Meditation tends to be more active mentally than contemplation.

Contemplation, on the other hand, is more like praying without using words. It's just being with God and enjoying His presence without saying anything. Another way to think of it is as admiring God without trying to analyze Him. We do this with friends as well: we don't always have to be doing or saying something when we are with them in order to be enjoying their company and growing in our relationship with them.

Another way to keep these two prayer methods straight is to remember meditation leans more towards analysis and application while contemplation leans more towards hanging out and just enjoying each other's company.

There is something else important to keep in mind when it comes to the distinction between vocal and mental prayer. Vocal prayers don't have to stay vocal but can ascend to mental prayer. What does that mean? You can meditate on the words of the Our Father. You can really meditate on the mysteries of the Rosary. Vocal prayers can be a springboard into mental prayer. Or they can stay vocal. It's more about the attitude with which you approach the prayer than whether words are involved or not.

Because vocal prayers tend to be easier for us, it's tempting to just add more and more vocal prayers in when we're trying to build our relationship with God. Vocal prayers aren't bad. They have their place. The problem is, very often, when we put too much emphasis on vocal prayer then we aren't giving room for God to speak to us. If you want to grow in prayer, just like if you want to grow in knowledge of any subject, you have to take on more difficult tasks. Keep it easy while working to build your prayer habit up but once you have the habit it's time to hone your skills. If you insist on only hanging out in the shallow end of the pool you aren't going to be able to swim in the deep end no matter how much time you've spent in the water.

If you've never tried meditation, start there. Try reading the daily Mass readings slowly for five or ten minutes. Put yourself in the scene you're reading about and try to see how it applies to your life right now. Talk to God about what's happening in the story or the area of your life that came to mind when you read the story. This is a stripped down form of Lectio Devina or meditating with scriptures.

Working mental prayer into your daily prayer routine can really help you to grow closer to God. Mental prayer tends to make it easier for us to share more of ourselves with God and to receive more of Him.

Don't let the prayer method constrict you

If you've been praying with a particular method for a long time you can get very attached to it. It's almost like a badge of honor. I have read my Bible every day for years! This kind of discipline is awesome. The question we need to ask, though, is if that way of prayer is still helping us to get in touch with God in a way where we're learning more about Him and He more about us.

Sometimes it's fun to try new things with people you know. If you always go to the coffee shop when you meet your friends you might have a great time, but then you also never get to see the other side of your friends which comes out when you're hiking together or going to the movies. It's not that it's a bad thing to have a regular coffee date with your friends. It's just that you might get to know them better if you try doing something new with them.

Relationships, even good ones, change over time. As relationships change so do methods of relating. This means that as you grow closer to God your prayer life should be changing. It's good to have a discipline of prayer but we also need to seek to grow in prayer.

We shouldn't be more attached to our prayer methods (or devotions) than we are to the one to whom they point. In fact, it's very easy for prayer methods to become an idol and an obstacle to our actual worship of God when we make devotion to them more important than devotion to Him whom they should be pointing us toward.

It's good to learn the method but we shouldn't let the method constrict us so much that it becomes the only way to pray. Try varying the methods of prayer you use if you've been using the same method for a while and you feel like something is missing. Keep in mind the goal is to get closer to God: to let Him know you better while you're getting to know Him better too.

Integrate new methods slowly and give them time to see if they are bearing fruit.

Don't do so much you forget to be

Sometimes we focus on the method so much we forget what we're actually doing. In other words, we are so busy paying attention to moving our lips that we forget to pay attention to God.

Our goal isn't to be the most accomplished person with the most brilliant insights gained during prayer. It's not to flaunt our knowledge of how to do things properly. We're trying to please God, not ourselves. We need to try not to get so busy doing prayer we forget to actually be with God while we're praying.

If you are trying to grow deeper in prayer it's a good idea to work some moments of silence into your prayer time. A few minutes a day to just sit with God is a good way to start if you aren't used to being silent during your prayer time. This is part of moving into contemplation and it's actually pretty hard. It's even harder than meditation.

Sometimes we get so busy wanting to do things for God (or in honor of God) we forget to just spend time with Him. We don't always have to be frantically running from place to place. We can just sit and rest with Him. We can 'waste time' with God and it's not actually wasted time during prayer. We don't always have to be doing or saying something to be spending quality time in the presence of God.

What if you've tried all of those things? Are you a prayer warrior who prays every day, does meditation, visits the Eucharist weekly or daily, and always strives to put your heart and mind behind your prayer? You can't possibly have hit your limit in getting closer to Him, have you? Is there really nothing else?

Instead of worrying about how well you're doing, ask yourself this: have I put God into a box? Do I only think about God during my prayer time? Try inviting the presence of God into every moment of your day. Don't keep Him in His regularly scheduled prayer time – although that's an awesome thing to have.

Part of growing in a relationship is being with people. It makes sense that if we want to grow closer to God we need to invite Him into more places in our life and day. But how do we do that?

There are a handful of methods which can be

used to do this. Perhaps one of the most well-known is the practice of offering something up. The something offered could be a task, a situation, or even a specific hour of your day. St Francis de Sales talks about this in his Spiritual Directory in a section called 'The Direction of Intention'.[3] He recommends making this offering to God before beginning any action. Essentially what you are doing is asking for God to be with you in each action as you are offering it to Him. This type of prayer is also sometimes known as Practicing the Presence of God from a little book of the same name by Brother Lawrence. Another way you can think of this spiritual habit is as trying to walk with Jesus in every moment instead of just keeping visiting hours with Him.

Remember, God is a gentleman and He doesn't come where He isn't wanted. If we invite Him into every moment we can make every moment a prayer. In that way we can, as St Paul exhorts us: *Rejoice always, pray constantly, give thanks in all circumstances; for this is the will of God in Christ Jesus for you. (1 Thess 5:16-18)*

---

[3] The Spiritual Directory is a rule of life used by some religious orders and can be accessed at: http://www.oblates.us/our-charism/spiritual-directory/

Ask Yourself:

1.) How would you describe your current prayer state (what you say, how often, with what kind of attention)?

2.) Do you like certain types of prayer more than others? Which ones do you like?

3.) Do you have moments of silence in your day?

Take Action:

1.) *Just starting out:* Pick one thing you can do for prayer every day for a week. Stick with it and be consistent. Check in at the end of the week and see how you did.

2.) *Going deeper:* If you are used to vocal prayer, pick something to meditate on (scripture, writings of the saints) and pray with that this week. Check in at the end of the week and see how you did.

4 - ASKING, SEEKING, AND KNOCKING

And I tell you, Ask, and it will be given you; seek, and you will find; knock, and it will be opened to you. For every one who asks receives, and he who seeks finds, and to him who knocks it will be opened. (Lk 11:9-10)

One type of prayer we're usually pretty good at is when we ask God to do things for us. Whether it's please-let-me-pass-this-test, please-bless-this-person, or something more serious we have all asked God for something at some point in our lives.

Asking God for things falls under a type of praying called "petitions" or "intercession." We ask God to bless us and to give us good things at every Mass, and petitions generally form a good part of our prayer time away from Mass. We know God is our Father, and kids don't normally have any problems asking their parents for things. God even tells us in the Bible that we're supposed to ask Him for things. We aren't imposing on Him when we come to Him with our petitions.

Unlike some of the prayer types we talked about in the last chapter, petitions aren't an advanced skill we have to practice to be able to do well. It's easy to ask God for things whether you started praying yesterday or have been praying for years. We can easily misunderstand how petitions work, though, even though we're good at making them. This can damage our relationship with God so it's a good idea to examine our attitude towards God and prayer when it comes to intercessions.

If you've ever asked God for something you've probably noticed you don't always get what you asked for. The same thing happened with our parents when we were kids. You can ask, plead, or try to strike a bargain but sometimes you just don't get what you want. Why don't we always get what we want when we ask for it? Why would God not give us the things we ask for if they are good things?

It's easy to get discouraged when God doesn't give us what we ask for. We can start to think God doesn't listen to us or maybe that He doesn't care about us that much. This can be especially hard if we see other people getting what they're praying for while we're either still waiting for an answer or know for sure that we aren't going to get what we wanted.

One thing we have to keep in mind about prayer is that all prayer is just talking to God. Whenever we talk to God, whatever we're talking about, we're building or maintaining relationship with Him. Prayer isn't a magic formula where if I say a prayer exactly the right way than I'll get exactly what I want from God.

We know God is our loving father. One of the things loving fathers want is to give their children good things. God tells us about this in the Gospel of Matthew: *If you then, who are evil, know how to give good gifts to your children, how much more will your Father who is in heaven give good things to those who ask him! (Mt 7:11)*

The good news is that God wants to give us good things! We can better understand this, though, as God wanting not just to give us good things but also things which are good for us. Those two things can be different, and this is one place we can get confused about. Just because something is good (and we want it) doesn't mean it's actually good for us to have.

It's often easier for us to tell whether something is good or bad in and of itself then it is for us to tell if it's good or bad for us to have it. God is omniscient—which means He knows everything—so He knows what we need and what's good for us to have. He also knows what we want and need before we ask for it, but He likes to be asked. That's why, even though God is omniscient, He tells us to ask Him for the things we want and need and we make prayers of petition.

When God responds to our prayers of petition it's generally in one of three ways: "Yes", "Not That Way", or "No." We'll talk about each of these responses more in the sections below.

"Yes": The story of Bartimaeus

There are quite a few stories about prayer in the Bible. The first one we're going to look at is about Jesus healing a blind man named Bartimaeus:

And they came to Jericho; and as he was leaving Jericho with his disciples and a great multitude, Bartimaeus, a blind beggar, the son of Timaeus, was sitting by the roadside. And when he heard that it was Jesus of Nazareth, he began to cry out and say, "Jesus, Son of David, have mercy on me!" And many rebuked him, telling him to be silent; but he cried out all the more, "Son of David, have mercy on me!" And Jesus stopped and said, "Call him." And they called the blind man, saying to him, "Take heart; rise, he is calling you." And throwing off his cloak he sprang up and came to Jesus. And Jesus said to him, "What do you want me to do for you?" And the blind man said to him, "Master, let me receive my sight." And Jesus said to him," Go your way; your faith has made you well." And

*immediately he received his sight and followed
him on the way. (Mk 10:46-52)*

Did you notice any of these things when you
were reading the story?

- Bartimaeus got what he asked Jesus for: his
  sight.
- Bartimaeus had to ask several times before he
  got what he wanted. People were even telling
  him to be quiet and quit asking.
- Bartimaeus ended up being closer to Jesus
  after he got what he was asking for.

Take a moment to read through the story again
and see if you can pick out anything else you
didn't notice the first time.

Sometimes when we ask God for something He
answers us with "Yes" and gives us exactly what
we were asking for. We like hearing "Yes"
whether it's God or someone else speaking. It's
easier for us to love God and feel close to Him
when He is giving us what we want.

Even if God is going to tell us "Yes" to a request,
though, more often than not we don't get what
we're asking for right away. Bartimaeus sure
didn't. He cried out several times before Jesus
called him over. The same thing is true for us: we
often have to ask for something more than once
before we get it. One thing Jesus tells us, and we

see it in this story of Bartimaeus, is to persist in prayer.

Keep asking! Don't give up if you don't get what you are asking for right away. It isn't that God doesn't hear you: He does. He wants to be in relationship with us, though, not just a vending machine which dispenses whatever we want whenever we want it.

Something else happens in the story of Bartimaeus which isn't explained. When Jesus calls him, Bartimaeus leaves his place by the roadside to come closer to Him. But how does a blind man find another man in a whole crowd of people? The Bible says there was a great multitude there on the road with Jesus. So how did Bartimaeus get from the side of the road to the side of Jesus through all of those people who were in between them?

It's likely that the people in the crowd helped Bartimaeus get closer to Jesus. The same thing is true for us. Often when we ask God for something other people help us out when God says "Yes" to what we are asking for. God likes to minister to us through other people. This doesn't mean God isn't involved in our lives when He chooses to work this way. God wants to be with us. He wants to be with us so much He chooses to work through us to help others get closer to Him.

Why did Jesus ask Bartimaeus to come closer? We know from other stories in the Bible Jesus doesn't have to be physically close to people in order to heal them. There are two interesting points here in the fact Jesus calls Bartimaeus closer. First, it seems like Jesus wanted to be closer to Bartimaeus at that moment. Second, it also seems like Jesus wanted Bartimaeus to participate in what was about to happen.

Jesus wanted Bartimaeus to come closer to Him and speak with Him. He didn't do this so He could place demands or conditions on Bartimaeus in order for him to receive his sight. We know from the story that after his healing Bartimaeus freely choose to follow after Jesus. Notice, Jesus never told him he had to come along. Bartimaeus got closer to Jesus through asking for his sight and then he decided to stay closer to Jesus once he was there.

Bartimaeus had to move from the side of the road to get closer to Jesus, though. Sometimes we also have to take action to get what we are asking for. This doesn't mean God isn't doing anything or that He doesn't want us to have what we're asking for. It means He wants us to participate. He wants us to engage with Him faithfully and trustingly. When He says "Yes" that sometimes means we have to take action in order to receive the "Yes" He is giving us.

In the scripture verse we began the chapter with, Jesus tells us to ask, seek, and knock in our prayer. Notice, all of these are action phrases. Jesus wants us to be close to Him and He wants to give us good things. This means we sometimes have to take action in order to be ready to receive the good things He wants to give us.

Sometimes, though, God doesn't give us exactly what we were asking for when He answers our prayer. This is the answer "Not That Way."

"Not That Way": The story of the lame beggar

Why wouldn't God give us something we want when we ask for it? It's usually because it either isn't good for us to have or He has something better in mind that He wants to give us instead.

We see this happen in the next Bible story we're going to look at. In this story, God works through St Peter to heal a lame beggar who wasn't even asking for healing:

> *Now Peter and John were going up to the temple at the hour of prayer, the ninth hour. And a man lame from birth was being carried, whom they laid daily at that gate of the temple which is called Beautiful to ask alms of those who entered the temple. Seeing Peter and John about to go into the temple, he asked for alms. And Peter directed his gaze at him, with John, and said, "Look at us." And he fixed his attention upon them, expecting to receive something from them. But Peter said, "I have no silver and gold, but I give you what I have; in the name of Jesus Christ of Nazareth, rise and walk." And he took him by the right hand and raised him up; and immediately his feet and ankles were made*

strong. And leaping up he stood and walked and entered the temple with them, walking and leaping and praising God. And all the people saw him walking and praising God, and recognized him as the one who sat for alms at the Beautiful Gate of the temple; and they were filled with wonder and amazement at what had happened to him. (Acts 3:1-10)

Did you notice these things when you were reading the story?

- The lame beggar asked for money.
- St Peter didn't have any money, and instead prayed for healing for the beggar.
- After the beggar was healed he was really happy even though he didn't get what he asked for.

Go back and read through the story again and see what else you notice.

The lame beggar, like Bartimaeus the blind beggar, was persistent in asking for what he wanted. He was by that gate asking for money every day. It's not a bad thing for us to ask God for what we need or want. It's also not a bad thing for us to persist in asking God for things we need or want.

One thing we need to understand about petitions is that if we ask God for something and He gives us something else instead that doesn't automatically mean what we were asking for was bad or bad for us. It's not that the beggar didn't need money. In fact, he probably still needed money after he finished leaping and praising God because he could walk. It's okay for us to ask God to provide for our material needs and wants as well as our spiritual needs and wants. We don't have to limit ourselves in what we ask Him for.

When we ask God for something, though, we need to do it with the expectation we're going to receive something. Why would we ask for something if we didn't think we were going to get it? Sometimes we bring this attitude to prayer: I'm going to ask even though I don't think God will hear me or do anything about it so that at least I can say I asked. Whenever we come to God with our petitions we need to be confident He is going to give us something. We also need to trust that what He gives us is going to work for our good.

One thing this story makes clear is that the beggar was asking Peter and John for money expecting to receive something. Beggars never know how much they are going to get when someone reaches into their pocket or purse. The beggar asked with the hope he would get something from them, even though he wasn't asking for a specific amount. It's possible the only reason the beggar was healed that day was because he was asking for a good thing (money) and God decided to give him something better instead (the ability to walk). He might never have received the ability to walk if he wasn't asking for money.

What the story doesn't say is that the beggar was bummed out because St Peter didn't pray to God for him (the beggar) to be blessed with money every time he sat by the gate and begged. The beggar was happy with what God gave him even though he had maybe never thought to ask for that thing.

You may also have noticed that, unlike in the story of Bartimaeus, we don't know what happens to the lame beggar after he's healed. What becomes of him? It's implied the beggar no longer gets his money by begging. He is going to have to do something else to make his living now that he can walk. This means his way of life is radically changed, but we don't know how. Notice, St Peter didn't tell him to go and do anything particular—he said "Rise and walk!" The beggar has to figure out what he's going to do with the gift God has given him.

This is something which can also be true for us. Sometimes the good thing God gives us also brings us a new set of challenges. We see an example of this in the story of the announcement the angel Gabriel gives to Mary at the beginning of the Gospel of Luke. Mary received a good thing: the news she would be the mother of God. That good thing didn't also come with a set of plans or additional guidelines for how to proceed now that everything in her life was going to be different. It also brought along with it some new challenges and difficulties Mary wouldn't have had to face otherwise: the flight into Egypt to escape Herod and the passion and death of her son.

Just because these new challenges presented themselves it did not mean that what Mary received was bad. What she received was good. The same thing is true for us. Just because the good we receive brings new challenges for us that does not mean it was not good or it was not ours to receive. It just means that sometimes we get a good we did not expect in answer to our prayers and that that good can bring with it a new set of circumstances in which God is going to pour Himself out to us. We may not get the whole answer at once. God does not leave us to figure it out alone, though. He continues to walk with us.

Some important things we can learn about prayer from this story of the lame beggar are that although God answers our petitions He doesn't always answer them by giving us exactly what we were asking for. He doesn't always give us a blueprint for what we're supposed to do with the answer He does give us. We also need to ask with the expectation of receiving something. In cases where He gives us an answer we weren't expecting, we need to stay in communication with Him to figure out how to respond to what He does give us.

This response of "Not That Way" to our petitions can be exciting when the answer we get is something which is obviously better than what we were asking for. God's response can become quite difficult to hear, however, if He tells us not "Yes" and not "Not That Way" but instead "No."

"No": The story of Gethsemane

Sometimes God doesn't seem to hear us when we pray. This can be really hard to deal with, especially if you're praying for something you really want.

That's not even the worst-case scenario in our eyes. Sometimes when we pray for things God says "No," without bothering to tell us why He's telling us "No." We are then left to deal with the fact we aren't going to get what we want and we don't know why.

It's not just to us that God says "No," though. Even Jesus, God's only son, was told "No." On the eve of His passion, Jesus travels with His disciples to the garden of Gethsemane. He prays very earnestly for the suffering of His crucifixion and death to be taken away from Him:

And he came out, and went, as was his custom, to the Mount of Olives; and the disciples followed him. And when he came to the place he said to them, "Pray that you may not enter into temptation." And he withdrew from them about a stone's throw, and knelt down and prayed, "Father, if you are willing, remove this chalice from me; nevertheless not my will, but yours, be done." And there appeared to him an angel from heaven, strengthening him. And being in an agony he prayed more earnestly; and his sweat became like great drops of blood falling down upon the ground. And when he rose from prayer, he came to the disciples and found them sleeping for sorrow, and he said to them, "Why do you sleep? Rise and pray that you may not enter into temptation." While he was still speaking, there came a crowd, and the man called Judas, one of the Twelve, was leading them… Then they seized him and led him away, bringing him into the high priest's house. (Lk 22:39-47a, 54a)

Did you notice any of these things when you read the story?

- Jesus asked for something specific, but He also said "not my will, but yours, be done."
- Jesus did not get what He asked for.
- Jesus was stressing over what the answer to His prayer was going to be.
- God sent an angel to strengthen Jesus even though the answer to His request was "No."

Go back and read through the story again and see if you can pick out anything else you didn't notice the first time.

God tells us that it's okay to ask Him for things. When tells us that it's okay for us to ask Him for things, He doesn't guarantee that just because we

ask for something we will get what we asked for.
Sometimes God tells us "No" when we ask for
something good, something which we think
would make us happy, because He has a different
plan for us.

It's important to note that even though Jesus
asked for something specific He also put that
request under the Father's will. By saying "not my
will, but yours, be done" He was telling God that
He was willing to accept an answer of "No" to His
request.

Why would Jesus do that? Especially here,
where He was worried about having to go
through what He knew was coming, why would
Jesus not demand God give Him exactly what He
was asking for?

The answer lies in the intimacy of Jesus'
relationship with the Father. Jesus trusted God
totally and completely. He trusted God to the
point of laying down His life when it was asked of
Him. Jesus knew that whatever the Father willed
at any moment was for the best even if it hurt to
receive the Father's will. By submitting His
request to the Father, Jesus was saying He trusted
in the Father's plan. In Gethsemane, that plan
meant Jesus didn't get the answer "Yes" to His
request for the cup of suffering to pass Him by.

This brings us to another important point. Just
because we don't get something we asked for
doesn't mean we were asking for something that
was bad for us to have. In Gethsemane, Jesus

knew there was a lot of suffering coming His way. Not just any suffering, but really bad suffering which was going to end in His death.

We know if Jesus hadn't died on the cross for our sins than we wouldn't have been saved. If Jesus had not gone through the suffering of His passion and death than we would not be able to be with God forever in heaven. God knew that too. So when Jesus asked for the chalice to pass from Him, the Father's will in that instance was "No, the chalice shall not pass." This was because He knew that if it did pass than the better thing He planned to give us would not be possible.

Whenever we come to God asking for something we want or need it can be frustrating, or even heartbreaking, when God tells us "No." We know God is our Father who wants to give us good things. That's why it can be so hard to accept when God tells us "No," especially when the thing we were asking for was good in and of itself. If God tells us "No" and we then get angry at God and stay angry at Him that is damaging to our relationship with Him. It's important to understand that sometimes God is going to tell us "No" even though He loves us.

God's love for us does not involve us getting everything we want. God has a plan and a purpose for our lives which ultimately is for us to be with Him forever in Heaven. God did not create us just so He could have someone to make miserable for no good reason on the elusive promise of one day achieving happiness for putting up with all of that suffering. God is a loving father, not a sadistic torturer.

We often misunderstand what love is, though. Love does not mean I give the other person everything that they want. Love means that I desire the good of the other. Sometimes desiring the good of the other means they don't get what they want. You may have heard the saying "love hurts" or "tough love." Sometimes we focus on this more from the side of the giver: that sometimes it can hurt to give love to someone else because we have to sacrifice our own good. The opposite side to this is also true: when someone, acting out of love for us, doesn't give us what we want it really hurts to receive that love.

God knows whether the thing we are asking for fits in with our ultimate wellbeing. If what we are asking Him for does not fit with this than He is not going to give it to us when we ask for it even if we really want it. God loves us and this means He will give us what is best for us. This also means sometimes He tells us "No" when we ask for something because while it might bring us happiness in the short-term in the long-term it will not satisfy.

Let's say you are a small child, perhaps 2-3 years old, enjoying a summer's day at the beach. After a long day playing in the sand and the sun you are very thirsty. There is plenty of water in the ocean and so you go to get a drink from the waves crashing on the shoreline. Your father, who has been nearby watching the whole time, shouts at you "No, don't drink that water!" In your current very thirsty state even though you know the water is salty you still want to drink it. You don't understand why your father would shout "No!" at you when you are so thirsty.

Your father knows that if he lets you drink the seawater you are going to be even thirstier than you would be if you hadn't. So, even though you really want it, he tells you "No" for your own good. You don't understand, and your father doesn't shout a long explanation at you when he tells you "No." Him telling you "No" is the loving response in this situation even though you are thirsty and the seawater is right there.

The answer of "No" can be hard to accept. Sometimes a loving Father tells us "No," because He knows it's better for us not to have what we are asking for. This doesn't mean He is just dismissing us and not listening when we ask for things. He is listening. He doesn't only have His eyes on our future happiness either, although it might sound that way. God cares about us in a daily, moment-to-moment kind of way which includes our past, present, and future.

Notice, even though God did not spare His Son from suffering and death on a cross, He did do something else for Him in that moment when He was praying in the garden. Even though Jesus received the answer "No" He also received help in the form of an angel who was sent to strengthen Him for what was to come. God wasn't going to take the cross away. Instead, He gave Jesus the strength He needed to bear it. God always hears us when we pray. If we pray expecting to receive something from God we will receive something. The something we receive, however, will not always be the something we expect.

Wait—I'm confused!

How do we know which answer we're getting from God (Yes, Not That Way, No) when we've been praying for something and nothing seems to be happening? And why should we ask God for things if He already knows whether He's going to give it to us or not?

Asking God for the things we want and need is the first step in a conversation with Him about what we are desiring. This is one of the ways we can grow in our relationship with God. We said earlier that intimacy in relationships is about how much of ourselves we share with another person and how much of themselves that person shares with us. When we speak to God about our desires we are being open and vulnerable with God about what we want. This openness is a move towards greater intimacy and it helps our relationship with Him to grow stronger.

God knows what we want and what we need before we say anything to Him about it. When we go to God with the things we want, that gives us a chance to hear what He has to say to us about our desires. God speaks to us in conversation. We'll talk more about listening to what God has to say to us in the next chapter. For now, keep in mind prayer and relationships are not supposed to be one-sided. Both people have a role to play.

Asking for what we desire also helps us to see where our heart is in relation to God. If you are asking God for something bad to happen to that person who hurt you today—well, God loves that person and desires their good too. If we are trying to build a relationship with God, we have to be careful not to bring anything into that relationship which is going to pull us further away from God. We don't want to damage our relationship with God by bringing bad things into it. Asking God for something gives us time to have that conversation with Him about whether that something is good for our relationship with Him or not.

God also may not give us things if we ask for them for the wrong reasons. If you are only asking for something so you can use it to sin with than God knows it isn't good for you to have. If we decide it's more important for us to have that something than it is for us to be close to God than that indicates a major red flag in the relationship. It's something which will need to be addressed in order for the relationship to continue to mature.

How are we going to know which answer we're getting (Yes, Not That Way, or No) when we pray? This is where discernment comes in.

Some people say there is a fourth way God answers our prayers: "Not yet." God wants the soil of our hearts to be ready to receive the good things He is going to plant in them. Our wants and desires can get ahead of our ability to receive what we want and desire, though. Sometimes God is going to tell us "Yes" but the timing isn't right for us to receive it, and so the answer we get is "Not yet."

God wants us to be persistent in asking Him for things even if it seems like we aren't getting an answer. Sometimes our desires can get ahead of our ability to receive what we are desiring. Our persistence in the desire for something can help us to be ready to receive what we desire. We see persistence as a major theme in Bible stories about prayer, including some of the ones we looked at above. Another story Jesus tells his disciples is about the Widow and the Judge:

> *And he told them a parable, to the effect that they ought always to pray and not lose heart. He said, "In a certain city there was a judge who neither feared God nor regarded man; and there was a widow in that city who kept coming to him and saying, 'Vindicate me against my adversary.' For a while he refused; but afterward he said to himself, 'Though I neither fear God nor regard*

*man, yet because this widow bothers me, I will
vindicate her, or she will wear me out by her
continual coming.'" And the Lord said, "Hear
what the unrighteous judge says. And will not
God vindicate his elect, who cry to him day and
night? Will he delay long over them? I tell you,
he will vindicate them speedily. Nevertheless,
when the Son of man comes, will he find faith on
earth?" (Lk 18:1-8)*

Did you notice these things when you were
reading the story?

- The widow kept hearing the judge say "No"
- The widow kept asking, and even made a
  nuisance of herself!
- The judge eventually gave her what she was
  asking for.

When we come to God in prayer we have to
have faith. We have to trust God is going to give
us what is good for us. We have to be persistent in
asking. God doesn't mind if we nag Him. In fact,
He pretty much tells us to.

God wants us to "Ask, Seek, Knock" in our
prayer time. This means we shouldn't be afraid to
ask Him for things we want, ask persistently, and
then be ready to participate in what He gives us in
return.

Ask Yourself:

1.) Did you ever pray really hard for something and not get it?

2.) Did you ever pray for one thing and then receive something else? Did the something else end up being better or worse for you?

3.) Have you been praying for something for a long time and you aren't sure what answer you're getting?

Take Action:

1.) List three things you want. Present them to God in prayer and, following Jesus' example, ask for His will to be done regarding those things.

5 - DID YOU SAY SOMETHING?

And the LORD came and stood forth, calling as at other times, "Samuel! Samuel!" And Samuel said, "Speak, for your servant hears." (1 Sam 3:10)

Learning how to pray well is more than just getting into the habit of praying every day. Prayer is speaking with God. Usually when we think about prayer we spend a lot of time thinking about what we're going to say. Speaking with someone isn't just one person talking, though. In order for our relationship with God to grow we need to learn not only how to talk to Him but also how to listen to Him too.

In the first chapter, we talked about how God wants a covenant with us. Covenants are exchanges of persons and not exchanges of services like contracts are. It's hard to exchange persons with someone else when you're the only one doing all of the talking. That's a very one-sided relationship. To get better at prayer and to grow closer to God we need to learn how to listen when we pray.

This might seem strange to you if you've grown up with the idea that 'reciting' your prayers is all there is to it. When we recite our prayers we're the only one talking at that moment. God wants to speak to us, but we won't be able to hear Him if we aren't giving Him a chance to speak.

Before we move into how to better listen to God when He speaks, let's look at a few things we need to understand in order to prepare ourselves to hear Him better.

You don't have to look too far in the Bible before you come across stories about God speaking to His people. There is the story of Moses and the burning bush in Exodus, there is the story of King Solomon asking God for wisdom in the book of Kings, and there is the story of Joseph being warned in a dream to flee to Egypt in the Gospel of Luke to name just a few. God has definitely spoken to His people in the past. Just because we read stories about God speaking to people in the past, though, doesn't mean we're quick to believe He still wants to speak to us now. Does God speak to us today? More importantly, does 'us' include you?

Yes, God wants to talk to you! Remember, He wants to be close to His people. He wants a relationship with them. That doesn't mean He's like that distant relative who only wants to hear from you at Christmas when the letter summarizing everything from the last year arrives. God wants to be involved in your daily life and that means He wants to speak to you in the here and now as you are experiencing it.

In order to hear God better we need to work on getting to the point where we believe God can and will speak to us. It's really hard to hear someone if you aren't listening. We need to come to prayer with the expectation God has something to say to us. When we have that expectation we're taking the first step towards being able to hear Him.

There're lots of reasons why we choose to talk to the people around us. Sometimes we want to get to know them better, to catch up, or even just to get information we need. There can be lots of reasons God would choose to talk to us too. Probably the most important one is that God loves us. He wants to be with us and to put a share of His divine life in us. One of the ways that happens is through prayer.

At this point you might be wondering how badly God actually wants to speak to us. I mean, if He really wants to so badly, why aren't angels gliding into our rooms with divine tidings all the time? Even if He wasn't so dramatic about it, why haven't you heard Him speak to you before if He's so eager to talk to you?

Part of the answer to this has to do with whether we are listening for God to speak or not. If you aren't listening for Him to speak than how are you going to hear Him when He does?

Let's say you're standing across the room from someone who wants to talk to you. Maybe you're at a party and other people are talking so it's pretty noisy. How loudly does the person across the room have to speak so you can hear them? Probably pretty loudly. He may even have to shout to get your attention. How much do you think he's going to be able to tell you if he has to shout? Maybe something short. That's a really hard way to communicate, though. You certainly wouldn't want to talk about something serious or personal if you had to shout across a noisy room at each other. You'd probably rather go somewhere quieter where you can hear each other better.

There's a story in the first book of Kings about the prophet Elijah meeting God on the mountain of Horeb. Elijah had just been through an epic showdown with the prophets of the false god Baal where he slaughtered 450 of them (1 Kings 18:20-40). This made Queen Jezebel mad, and she said she was going to kill Elijah for it and so he ran away. Elijah ends up at Mount Horeb where this happens:

*And he said, "Go forth, and stand upon the
mount before the LORD." And behold, the LORD
passed by, and a great and strong wind tore the
mountains, and broke in pieces the rocks before
the LORD, but the LORD was not in the wind; and
after the wind an earthquake, but the LORD was
not in the earthquake; and after the earthquake a
fire, but the LORD was not in the fire; and after
the fire a still small voice. And when Elijah heard
it, he wrapped his face in his mantle and went out
and stood at the entrance of the cave. (1 Kings
19:11-13)*

Elijah recognized the still, small voice belonged
to God. Even though the wind, earthquake, and
fire were flashy and powerful Elijah knew God
wasn't in them. He also wasn't sitting at the
mouth of the cave straining really hard to hear
what God might say. We don't have to strain or sit
for hours and hours trying to hear what God has
to say. In fact, you are more likely to start hearing
things which aren't there if you do. It's like when
you start feeling you are able to hear the silence
itself when you are in a quiet room.

Listening is something which happens when we
are attentive for the other person to speak. Being
attentive doesn't require us to strain to hear. It is
us quieting ourselves enough to notice when
someone else says something. We can also be
listening even if the other person isn't saying

anything at the moment because listening is just being attentive to the other.

Just like you don't constantly shout at your friends when you're talking to them, God doesn't usually shout at us either. He wants to be close and He likes to speak to us personally. We can miss this if we aren't paying attention. We can also miss it if we're only expecting God to speak in flash and dazzle or shouting. More often, like with Elijah, He uses a still, small voice.

Scripture uses the word 'voice' to describe when God speaks. Because of this sometimes when we listen for God to speak we expect it to be an actual voice which materializes and speaks to us. More likely than not, when God speaks it won't be in an obviously supernatural way. Remember, we don't have angels gliding into our rooms all the time to deliver divine messages. What exactly does listening in prayer mean, then, if it's not straining to hear an actual voice?

You may have run across the terms 'God Coincidence' or 'a God thing.' These are phrases people use sometimes to describe when they believe God is saying something to them. They see the hand of God moving in the circumstances and events of their lives. For instance, a few years ago I was doing research on the Holy Spirit. One of my coworkers, who liked to tease me but who had no idea about my current project, one day greeted me by saying "I'm going to tell your mother you believe in the Holy Spirit." Since that wasn't remotely related to anything we had talked about before, or even something usual to say, I was very surprised. I took it as a possible nudge from God to continue paying attention to my research.

Notice, I wasn't straining to hear if God was going to say something to me at that moment. What I thought was God speaking to me also wasn't something which indicated I was supposed to do anything in particular. It was more like a nudge, something which you notice as part of a conversation but which isn't a life-altering command. Even though in the Bible the stories which are recorded often do involve life-changing commands or pronouncements, if you look at the everyday conversations you have with people you will notice this isn't how they normally go. Daily conversations tend to revolve more around sharing with and noticing what the other person is doing. So conversations tend to go more like this: "You have a test tomorrow? Tell me more about that." Or, "You won your game? That's great!"

Another thing we don't do in daily conversations is constantly go up to people and ask "Did you say something?" or "Was that you speaking?" We can be attentive to what is happening around us without always being on high alert for a signal to come in.

We also don't need to run every single coincidence or blip we come across on our radar through intense scrutiny so as to wring any possible meaning out of it. That would be an awful way to communicate with people. If God wants to bring something up, He isn't going to make you jump through a thousand hoops to figure it out. Like most people when they take the time to talk to you, God speaks to be understood. The more you have to strain and stress to pull a message out of something, the less likely it becomes there is actually anything there.

Another way God can speak to us is through inspirations or desires. Sometimes we get an idea to do something or a flash of insight into how to handle a particular situation and that's actually God giving us a little nudge. Maybe you were reading the Bible and felt really inspired by something you found there. Or maybe you keep running across the same idea or word over and over in different places. These are all ways God can choose to bring up something He wants us to pay attention to. We also have random thoughts and weird dreams sometimes. We've all had thoughts like, "I wonder what would happen if..." and we've all had the dream of falling where we wake up just before we hit the ground. Just because you had a thought or a dream, even if it keeps coming back around, doesn't automatically mean God is speaking to you.

How are you going to know if it might be God speaking or just you thinking?

Perhaps one of the most important things to keep in mind is that we must be careful not to place absolute certainty on anything before we see the fruit. Just because you had an inspiration or a good thought does not mean for sure it was God. Most of the time we cannot be absolutely certain. This is one of the reasons why when people feel a calling to a particular vocation there is a period of discernment they go through where the calling is tested out before it becomes a permanent vocation. Part of being a good listener is confirming that what you think you heard the other person say is actually what they said. This can take time, so it's important to be patient.

Maybe you're willing to admit God wants to speak to us and that 'us' includes you. The question still remains: how are you going to recognize if it might be God speaking to you? The rest of this chapter will focus on a few things you can do to help you learn how to better recognize when God might be speaking to you.

Spend time with the shepherd

Imagine your phone rings. You look at the caller ID before you answer and see it's your best friend. You answer the phone, but instead of hearing your best friend's voice you hear the voice of a stranger. The first thing you probably want to know is who this stranger is and how they got a hold of your best friend's phone.

Now imagine your phone rings and it's the repair shop you dropped your computer off at a few weeks ago. You answer the phone but, unless you know the guy who works there outside of dropping off your computer that one time, how are you going to know if the voice on the other end of the line belongs to the guy at the repair shop or not? You only talked to him once and that was a few weeks ago.

The more time we spend with someone the easier it is to recognize their voice and know it's actually them talking to us. If you hardly ever talk to someone it's a lot harder—or even impossible— to tell if it's them speaking to you or someone else.

If we want to be better able to recognize the voice of God when He speaks to us we need to spend time with Him in prayer, especially with the scriptures. All of scripture is inspired by God, so no matter which book of the Bible is your favorite you're getting more familiar with what God's voice sounds like when you read it.

One of the prayer methods mentioned in the chapters above was called Lectio Devina. This method of prayer involves reading and meditating on scripture. It's a good way to work scripture into your prayer time. One of the steps the method uses involves paying attention for any words or phrases in the passage being read to "jump out" in a new way. It may be a passage you have read many times before but this time a certain word or phrase just sticks out to you. This can be one way God speaks to us through scripture: by asking us to pay attention to something we hadn't noticed before.

If you pray with scripture frequently, or if you have a strong familiarity with scripture, you may also notice different verses come to mind while you are doing something else. These can be like the notes some kids find slipped into their lunch box which wish them a good day or good luck. The notes don't ask for anything in particular; they are just reminders the other person is there and cares. It's another way of sharing in the daily life of the person.

Another way to learn how God speaks is to read about the lives of the saints. Many of the saints had relationships with God where the stories we know about them include conversations they had with God: St Teresa of Avila, St Therese of Liseux, and St Faustina are just a few examples. Reading about how God has spoken to others in the past can also help you learn to recognize His voice when He speaks to you.

What's important here is our decision to be attentive to the other person when we are spending time with them. Just because we are listening does not automatically mean the other person will say something. It also doesn't mean that whatever is said will cause the course of our life to change dramatically right away. The more time we spend turning our hearts and minds towards God, the more listening opportunities we are creating by actively being with Him. This is definitely a step towards building a closer relationship with God. When we spend more quality time with someone, the quality of the relationship we can have with them grows.

Check for contradictions

Another way you can look for confirmation on whether your inspirations might be from God or not is to see if they contradict anything God has already revealed as true. We know from the Gospel of John that God is the source of all truth. Jesus tells His disciples: *I am the way, and the truth, and the life; no one comes to the Father, but by me. (Jn 14:6b)* If the truth contradicted itself it wouldn't really be true. Checking for contradictions can help us not only to learn more about what God has revealed in the past but also whether our inspirations might actually be God giving us a nudge.

One of the places we can find revealed truth is in the Bible. In fact, as St Paul reminds us:

All Scripture is inspired by God and profitable for teaching, for reproof, for correction, and for training in righteousness, that the man of God may be complete, equipped for every good work. (2 Tim 3:16-17).

Spending time with your Bible is a good way to learn more about what God has done and said.

Another place you can find revealed truth is in the teachings of the Catholic Church. Most Protestant churches believe in something called *solo scriptura.* This Latin phrase translates to "Scripture alone," which means they believe the truth of what Jesus taught can only be found in the Bible. Catholics don't believe in *solo scriptura.* They believe the truth of what Jesus taught is not only contained in the Bible but also in the sacred traditions and teachings which have been handed down faithfully over the years by the apostles. While the Protestants would say "Scripture only" the Catholics would respond with "Scripture and Sacred Tradition."

Sacred Tradition is also sometimes referred to as being part of the magisterium. "Magisterium" is a fancy word which means the teachings of the Catholic Church as handed down through the teaching authority of the bishops and popes. Sometimes these come out in the form of official documents such as encyclicals or letters from the pope to the bishops or lay faithful. There are over two hundred encyclicals which have been written and published and they cover a wide range of topics.

The Catechism of the Catholic Church, which is a summary of the teachings of the church on faith and morals, is another part of magisterial teaching which can be used to learn about revealed truth. It also has an excellent index in the back which lets you find passages related to specific topics quickly if you are looking for an answer dealing with a specific issue.

Sometimes having a reference guide or a textbook isn't enough, though. It's extremely hard to give one-size-fits all answers to the types of situations people find themselves in. We are all different people in the sense that the paths we walk towards God will go through different situations and experiences which we will need to respond to. No two people will have exactly the same experiences in life. Someone who is single will walk a different path than someone who is married or has chosen to enter religious life. Even within those categories, the challenges they face will not all be the same. While the broad principles can be found in the teachings of the church the application of those principles to specific situations can be more difficult to discern.

If you run across a situation where the answer isn't clear it's usually best to talk to someone with more knowledge in what you are dealing with. This is an experience we know from school. You can read the chapter and not understand it but when the teacher explains it, gives some examples, or connects it directly to your life it becomes much clearer. This is why one of the frequent recommendations made to people who believe God is calling them to religious life is to find a spiritual director.

A spiritual director is someone who can help you recognize where God might be moving in your life. It's not just for people discerning a call to religious life, either. Some people meet with a spiritual director regularly and some people go only when they have something specific they need help with. Sometimes a spiritual director might refer you to someone else, but good spiritual directors can be very helpful in checking for contradictions and learning how to listen to what God might be saying to you.

As you learn more about the truth from reading scripture, studying the teachings of the church, or having conversations with people who are strong in their faith you will grow in your ability to recognize the truth when you come across it. Knowing what the truth is makes it easier to recognize something false.

Check for a sense of peace or anxiety

If something is true and good does that automatically mean your inspiration was from God? If you've followed the first two guidelines you might feel like that's good enough to be sure. Keep in mind, though, we must be careful not to place absolute certainty on anything before we see the fruit. Another place we can check the fruit is by considering what our inner reaction to the inspiration is. Do we feel a sense of peace or a sense of anxiety when we think about acting on our inspiration?

Notice, I didn't say whether you felt like you really liked what you were hearing or not. That's a different question altogether. Sometimes God says things to us which we don't like, but which are true and good. An example would be doing something kind for that one person who has hurt you but who now needs your help. You probably don't feel warm and fuzzy about going to help them, but God might be inviting you to do that. So how do we understand the role of peace and anxiety when it comes to discernment?

A sense of peace can also be thought of as a sense of the rightness of doing a thing. We know from scripture God has good things He wants to give to us. He speaks about this in the Gospel of Luke when He asks what father would give their child bad things when they ask for good things. (Lk 11:11-13). One of the good things God likes to give us is confirmations when we start moving towards something He's inviting us to do. A confirmation is like a breadcrumb, a small positive sign, to tell us we are headed in the right direction. Having a sense of peace when we're thinking about doing something—even if it's something we don't want to do—can be a confirming sign.

A sense of anxiety about doing something, on the other hand, is more like a sense of dread or even 'heaviness' when you think about doing that thing. Anxiety is a bad thing. God does not have anxiety to give us. The first pope, St Peter, said in one of his letters: *Cast all your anxieties on him, for he cares about you. (1 Pet 5:7)* If we are feeling anxious we can be fairly sure the anxiety is not coming from God.

We still have to be careful, though, when it comes to discerning whether we have a sense of peace or anxiety about something. We can have a sense of peace something is the right thing to do but also have a sense of anxiety about actually doing the thing. This can be a common issue when God is inviting us to be better than what we currently are. Anxiety, in other words, can also ride on the top of a sense of peace and act as a distraction. It's one of the ways we can get tangled up in our thoughts when it comes to discernment.

Let's say you fall and break your leg. You have been petrified of going to the doctor since you were little, so the idea of going to get your leg put in a cast causes you great anxiety. Anxiety is not a good thing, so you might conclude you shouldn't go to the doctor. Deep down, though, you know if you want your leg to heal properly you have to go to the doctor and your leg healing properly is a good thing you desire. So what's the right thing to do? In this example, you need to go to the doctor so your leg can heal properly. There is a rightness to that decision even though you have to go through the anxiety of going to the doctor in order to accomplish it.

Sometimes getting past the sense of anxiety riding over the feeling of peace is extremely difficult. This is another good reason why we should allow ourselves time to discern those bigger inspirations. We should not feel rushed to take immediate action if we still feel the way forward is not clear. It's important to check whether the sense of peace is there before taking steps which have permanent consequences not just for ourselves but for others.

Testing the waters

If your inspiration sounds like God, doesn't contradict anything He's revealed in the past, and gives you a sense of peace when you think about it than it might be God speaking to you. The next thing you want to do is to test the waters. Start to take small steps towards fulfilling the inspiration. After you take the first small step check for more confirming signs. If the sense of peace stays than take another small step. If a sense of anxiety comes than stop and reflect again.

This process takes time. The larger the inspiration you are acting on is the longer you should expect to spend discerning if it's actually God speaking to you or not. Whether to hold the door open for a stranger at the store? No discernment required. Whether to quit your job and go be a missionary in a foreign country? You'll want to spend some time discerning that decision before you buy your plane ticket. Just because you aren't running out to buy a ticket immediately, though, doesn't mean you can't take other steps like talking to people who have done it before or gathering other information to help you make the decision.

If your inspiration is about something small than you can probably go through all of the discernment steps on your own. If you're trying to discern something big, though, it helps to get advice from someone who is wiser in spiritual matters than you are. This can be a good friend, a confirmation sponsor, or a spiritual director. It can also be arranging a short visit with one of your parish priests to talk things over.

Note though: when you seek out advice it's still your decision what to do. Seeking advice from others is not pushing the decision off onto someone else to let them make it for you. It's getting more data and feedback for your discernment process, not handing off the final say in the matter.

The key thing to remember is not to jump in with both feet. We need to be careful when acting on inspirations because God isn't the only one who likes to speak to us. It's said there are three sources of temptation: the world, the flesh, and the devil. These three things like to speak to us too, and they can be very subtle and quiet. Just because we are Christian and have said "Yes" to Jesus doesn't mean that every single thought or inspiration which pops into our heads is from Him. It's a good idea not to dive headfirst into the pool without checking how deep the water is.

Very often God will speak in generalities. For instance, in the story of the Annunciation, the angel Gabriel didn't give much instruction to

Mary as to what to do during the day now she was going to be the Mother of God. He gives her one little detail – your cousin Elizabeth is also pregnant—almost as an aside. Next thing we know, Mary has packed her bags and gone to the hill country to help her cousin. Did the angel tell her to go do that? No, he didn't. He brought the fact to her attention and Mary is the one who decided how to act on it.

You will almost never get an exact blueprint to follow along with your inspirations. God may be bringing something to your attention, but He very often leaves the choice of how to respond up to us. More inspirations may follow after the first small step is taken but the whole plan is almost never revealed to us all at once. This is why taking steps is so important when it comes to discerning whether God might be speaking to us or not. The farther you get along the path, the more is revealed.

All four of these things—spending time with the shepherd, checking for contradictions, checking for a sense of peace or anxiety, and testing what you hear—are part of good discernment. Discernment helps us to understand when God might be speaking to us. What do you do, though, if you think God might be speaking to you but you don't understand what He's saying?

The first step is to relax! God wants to be understood. We don't have a God who likes to confuse us. He doesn't spend all day devising puzzles for us just to see if we're smart enough or persistent enough to get what He's trying to tell us. He knows us better than we know ourselves and so He's going to speak to us in the ways we can understand Him.

It does sometimes happen, though, that God tells us something and we aren't sure exactly what He means by it. In fact, St Peter had this experience one time when he was praying:

"I was in the city of Joppa praying; and in a trance I saw a vision, something descending, like a great sheet, let down from heaven by four corners; and it came down to me. Looking at it closely I observed animals and beasts of prey and reptiles and birds of the air. And I heard a voice saying to me, 'Rise, Peter; kill and eat.' But I said, 'No, Lord; for nothing common or unclean has ever entered my mouth.' But the voice answered a second time from heaven, 'What God has cleansed you must not call common.' This happened three times, and all was drawn up again into heaven. At that very moment three men arrived at the house in which we were, sent to me from Caesarea. And the Spirit told me to go with them, making no distinction. These six brethren also accompanied me, and we entered the man's house… As I began to speak, the Holy Spirit fell on them just as on us at the beginning. And I remembered the word of the Lord, how he

said, 'John baptized with water, but you shall be
baptized with the Holy Spirit.' If then God gave
the same gift to them as he gave to us when we
believed in the Lord Jesus Christ, who was I that I
could withstand God?" (Acts 11:5-12, 15-17)

St Peter was pretty sure it was God talking to him in the story above. He wasn't quite sure what to make out of what God was saying, though. In fact, St Peter interpreted what was being said one way, pondered it, and then later realized that God also meant something else as well. God can do that—sometimes we won't understand what He's saying (or understand it fully) right away and that's okay.

We see this happen to us in our lives as well. Sometimes there's that phrase your parents always used to say. You knew it by heart because they said it so often. Then one day that phrase comes into your mind and you see a whole new meaning behind it which you hadn't seen when you were young. As we go through different experiences and grow in maturity we start to see things from a different perspective. This can happen when it comes to our conversations with God as well.

If you think God might be speaking to you but you aren't sure you understand what He's saying than you need to stay in dialogue with Him. God might be revealing something to you over time. He might be starting a conversation He means to continue for a while or even bringing something to your mind now so you'll remember it later when He's ready to say something more specific about it. You don't have to strain to hear Him or stress over trying to find every possible connection or coincidence which might make something make more sense. God wants to be understood and He does not purposefully make it hard for us to understand Him.

These extended conversations with God only happen if we're actively speaking and listening to Him, though. St Peter didn't throw His hands up in disgust and walk away from the vision even though he didn't understand what God was telling him. He stayed in dialogue with God about what He was saying and eventually it became clear to him. It wasn't that God wasn't speaking clearly or that St Peter wasn't listening hard enough. Instead, the message needed an extended conversation to show St Peter how God meant for it to be understood. St Peter had to be patient and wait as God developed the message over time.

These kinds of conversations can't happen if we are the only ones we allow to speak during our prayer time. We need to give time and space for God to speak to us and learn how to be quiet so we can patiently listen for what He has to say. This is also one of the reasons why the transition from vocal to mental prayer is so important for deepening your relationship with God. Mental prayer is more difficult but it also allows more space for God to speak to us during our prayer time.

Good relationships aren't just about asking for stuff. Good relationships are about sharing your life with the person you are building a relationship with. The kind of sharing that builds good relationships happens when both people are talking, not just one. We need to spend time listening to God when we come to Him in prayer.

Ask Yourself:

1.) Have you ever tried to be silent when praying? Do you find it easy or difficult?

2.) Have you ever asked God a question and then listened expecting an answer?

3.) What is your experience with discernment? Is it a comfortable thing to do or something you have to work at?

Take Action:

1.) Spend five minutes being quiet. Turn off your phone. Don't strain to hear anything, just practice being quiet.

2.) Ask God a question.

6 - WHO AM I?

Brethren, I do not consider that I have made it my own; but one thing I do, forgetting what lies behind and straining forward to what lies ahead, I press on toward the goal for the prize of the upward call of God in Christ Jesus. Let those of us who are mature be thus minded; and if in anything you are otherwise minded, God will reveal that also to you. (Phil 3:13-15)

One of the things great relationships have in common is that they grow and change as the people involved in them grow and change. Good relationships don't stay exactly the same as time goes by. Being in a relationship with someone, especially someone you're close to, changes you. Change itself isn't necessarily a bad thing. In fact, change is necessary in order for you and the relationship to thrive.

In a previous chapter, we talked about how your relationship with your best friend isn't the same today as it was the first day you met. Not only has your relationship changed, but you also aren't exactly the same person you were when the relationship started. The changes may be so small that when you look at them from day to day they are hardly noticeable. Over time, the effect of all those small changes adds up, though. As you grow and mature as a person, so do your relationships. And this is a good thing!

Growth and maturity aren't just about aging physically. There's also spiritual maturity which changes as we grow in our faith and our relationship with God deepens. St Paul talks about this in his letter to the Christians at Corinth, when he says: *When I was a child, I spoke like a child, I thought like a child, I reasoned like a child; when I became a man, I gave up childish ways. (1 Cor 13:11)* St Paul isn't just referring to the things children like to do such as play outside. He's referring to spiritual maturity, which is something we need to grow in to be able to follow Christ more closely each day.

When we think about what it means to be spiritually mature, we can go back to some of the things Jesus said about children and faith in the Gospels. Jesus is very welcoming to children. He even tells His disciples they need to come to Him

LIZ GARANT

like children (Mt 18:2-4). When we see passages
like this sometimes we can begin to think He
means we're supposed to come to Him acting like
children. This interpretation contradicts what St
Paul says about putting aside childish ways,
though. So what does Jesus mean when He says to
come to Him like children?

Jesus is asking for us to have a child-like faith.
The difference between having a child-like faith
and acting childishly is huge. A child-like faith
trusts completely in the Father. It's like the small
child who runs to his father after he scrapes his
knees expecting the father to know how to make it
better. A childish faith is immature in how it
relates to others, including God and ourselves. It's
more like the rebellious teenager throwing a
tantrum for not getting his way. Jesus is not telling
His disciples to come to Him childishly, striving to
remain immature in faith and how we love others.
Instead, He's asking His disciples to come to Him
with the full, loving trust which children have
towards their parents. A maturing faith is one
which is growing more child-like in its ability to
completely trust the Father.

The kind of relationship we can have with God
depends not only on what role we believe He
wants to play in our lives but also on the depth of
our spiritual maturity. We can see examples of this
in the parent-child relationships around us. An
infant or adolescent child does not have the same
kind of relationship with his parents that an adult

child does. If they did, we would think something was wrong. Our relationship with God will change as we grow in spiritual maturity and in our understanding of who God is. If we aren't maturing, though, our relationship with God can stagnate and that's not a good thing.

What does it mean for a relationship to stagnate? Stagnation in our spiritual life tends to happen when we get too comfortable with the way we are. We may even be doing lots of things for God (being involved in church, helping with some form of ministry, praying regularly, etc.) but still not be growing in our ability to trust God in those areas of our life where He wants to draw us closer to Him. The amount of spiritual activity we're involved in is not necessarily a sign of a healthy faith. This is true even though it's also true that a maturing faith can inspire us to greater activity in service of God.

God doesn't just want us to do things for Him. God wants us to do things with Him. It's very easy to become distracted by trying to do things for God and to forget to actually be with Him. If we ignore God and what He wants to do in our lives because we're so busy trying to do so many different things for Him than we're running the risk of missing out on what God actually wants.

God doesn't just want our sacrifices and works: He wants our hearts. He wants us to come to Him with what is in our hearts with a child-like trust in His ability to care for us. He wants us to draw closer to Him in an ever-deepening relationship. He wants to share more of Himself with us and to have us share more of ourselves with Him. If we're too comfortable with the way things are than we probably aren't as concerned with taking care of the things in our life which are keeping us from growing closer to God.

If we are striving to grow and mature in our faith than we can't just keep inside of our comfort zone when it comes to living our faith. It's the same as when you were in school. If you did the same math problems over and over again in class once you had learned to solve them, you would be spending your time doing math but you wouldn't necessarily be improving your ability to do math better. The same thing can happen in our spiritual life. If we don't practice our faith by trying to do the spiritual things which are harder for us than we're just treading water and not actually swimming.

In his epistles, St Paul likes to compare the Christian life to running a race. Preparing to run a race is a good analogy for spiritual growth. If you want to run the race well you're going to have to grow in speed (how fast you run) and endurance (how long you can run for). The way you grow in those areas is by practicing running faster and longer. To run faster or longer than you're used to is uncomfortable, and not just the first time you do it either. Every time you practice something to get better at it than you currently are it causes you to feel uncomfortable. If you don't push past that discomfort on the practice field, though, you won't grow in speed and endurance and you won't be able to run the race well.

One place we can work on growing in our spiritual maturity is by practicing the virtues. The Catechism of the Catholic Church tells us that "virtue is an habitual and firm disposition to do the good. It allows the person not only to perform good acts, but to give the best of himself." (CCC 1803) We need to practice in order to be able to give our best. Practicing virtue generally takes us outside of our comfort zone.

Whenever we think about virtues and vices, it's easier to understand the relationship between them if we picture a seesaw which has virtue on one end and vice on the other. As one end of the seesaw goes higher (gets stronger) the other end goes lower (gets weaker). The stronger the temptation to a vice you are facing the more opportunity there is to practice the opposing virtue. This means you have to work on the opposite end of the seesaw harder, though. The more you practice strengthening the opposite virtue the stronger your ability to resist the temptation to the vice gets. The seesaw doesn't move, though, unless some pressure is applied at one end or the other and that takes effort.

Sometimes when you listen to people talk about praying for a virtue you can come away confused about whether they actually want to grow in the virtue they are praying for or not. For instance, someone who is praying for patience may complain they will never pray for that virtue again because they end up having to wait everywhere they go! It's like they want to have the virtue, but not to ever have to use it. Their prayer request seems to be more about not being bothered or inconvenienced by those situations where they have to wait instead of actually getting the virtue of patience.

Every day is an opportunity to practice and grow in virtue. As you work on maturing spiritually you're going to come across new areas of weakness and new places where God is asking you to grow in order to achieve greater union with Him. This can be an uncomfortable experience, especially if you had the expectation of clearing the final hurdle in the race once you've strengthened a place you are currently struggling in.

The good news is God doesn't wait for us to be perfect to love us. He doesn't just care about us when our life is going perfectly. There will be some growing pains as we strive to mature spiritually. God works through those growing pains, though, to transform us into the saints He is calling us to be.

Remember how small changes over time lead to big changes? Those big changes are transformations. The transformation of a sinner into a saint is the end result of continual growth.

Our relationship with God should be one which transforms us from who we are today into the saint He is inviting us to be. That transformation doesn't happen without daily work at growth, though. If we want to be with God forever in Heaven than we need to cooperate with Him in the work He wants to do in us.

We aren't talking about just a superficial or surface transformation, either. The kind of transformation God wants to work in us goes deep and into every part of our lives. There is no part of your life the Holy Spirit does not want to help you to transform, to purify, and to make new.

Willingness to change

The closer you are to someone the greater impact they can have on your life. We say this about people all the time: "He really changed after he met his fiancée—it's like he's a different person!" The same thing can happen in our relationship with God. It should be such a significant thing in our life that it changes us in a way people can notice. The saints are great examples of how a continued relationship with God has a noticeable impact over a lifetime.

One important thing we have to have is a willingness to be changed. When we talked about growth, we said that growth means sometimes we have to get outside of our comfort zone. This means that growth, while good for us, isn't always a comfortable experience. If transformation is continual growth and growth is sometimes uncomfortable for us that means that our experience of transformation is not always going to be comfortable. Being willing to be changed means being willing to go through the discomfort of change in order to achieve a greater good.

Sometimes when you talk to Christians you can get the idea they think that just because they said "Yes" to Jesus their life is going to be easy now. That once you have Jesus in your life you don't suffer anymore and only good things will happen to you from that moment on. That if bad things are happening to you than you must not have really let Jesus into your life.

This is a very attractive lie. It's attractive because it's convincing and it's a lie because it is not true even though we would like for it to be true. Saying "Yes" to Jesus and becoming a Christian is not a ticket to a trouble-free life. The author of the New Testament tells us: *Count it all joy, my brethren, when you meet various trials, for you know that the testing of your faith produces steadfastness. (Jas 1:2-3)* The Bible is teaching us an important lesson we need to learn if we plan to continue as followers of Christ after saying "Yes" to Him.

Part of saying "Yes" to God is learning how to say it daily. We don't just say "Yes" once and then go on our way doing whatever we please, thinking we are following Jesus when we actually aren't. We have to say "Yes" daily. This means making the choice, daily, to stay with Him even when the going gets difficult and when trials or imperfections (great or small) crop up in our life.

Another part of saying "Yes" to God involves saying "No" to things which are not of God and pull us away from Him. It doesn't matter how much you like that other thing: if it isn't of God, you have to say "No" to it in order to be able to fully say "Yes" to what God has for you. We have to say "No" to these things even if they are things we really like. This is a conscious choice we have to make, not just something we fall into.

We can't fool ourselves into thinking God will let us bring the dirt of our sins, no matter how small they may seem to us, into Heaven like some kind of carry-on luggage we can check. God is light, and the light will drive out the dark. If you insist on hanging onto the dark than you will be driven away from Him along with the darkness you are choosing to hang onto.

Saying "Yes" to God is not a one and done event. This means that our experience of the transformation God wants to work in us will also not be a one and done event. The kind of growth which leads to transformation is about progress, not perfection. We should not get discouraged just because we are struggling with something. God wants to transform every area of our life. As we continue to grow in relationship with Him we are going to discover new places where we need His help and forgiveness. This doesn't mean we're a failure even if it feels like we're going backwards or not moving at all. Transformation is about staying with God even when the going gets tough and learning to trust Him even in those places where it's hard to do so.

We can see this kind of trust in the life of St Paul. The story of St Paul from the book of Acts begins when Paul's name was Saul. Saul was a zealous Jew intent on persecuting Christians. On his way to Damascus to continue the persecution there, he is blinded by a great light and a voice asks him: "Saul, why are you persecuting me?" When Saul asks who the owner of the voice is, the voice tells him: "I am Jesus, who you are persecuting." Saul continues on to Damascus where he is healed, receives his sight again, and goes to the nearest temple to begin proclaiming that Jesus is Lord. This is a radical transformation: Saul goes from persecuting Christians to being ready to be persecuted for being a Christian!

The story of Saul does not end there, though, with Saul running into the temple to proclaim "Jesus is Lord!" It was a noticeable shift from the way Saul was living to the way Paul was living. Paul still had to go through a lot of things before he went from being just Paul to being St Paul.

Paul doesn't have an easy life after he says "Yes" to Christ, either. If you keep reading in the book of Acts, he begins to talk about all these hardships he encounters. He's beaten, stoned, shipwrecked, lost at sea, and eventually he's martyred. All of this happens while he's out there trying to do the will of God and to be a good Christian. Saying "Yes" to God does not mean the end of our sufferings. If we look at the life of St Paul and the lives of the saints we see this is not the case. Suffering occurs; being Christian is not a guaranteed ticket to a life without any problems or suffering.

So how does Paul go from being just Paul to being St Paul? He perseveres through the difficulties he encounters on the way. He realizes it is in experiencing his weakness (whether physical or spiritual) and handing it over to Jesus that he is giving room for the transforming grace of God to work in his life. One of the most important things we can realize as a Christian is that in order to be Christian we have to stay with Jesus, persevering even when it's hard, trusting He is making something beautiful out of us even when it seems like everything is going wrong. We can't name ourselves Christian and then walk away from Christ when the going gets difficult and still be a follower of Christ. We have to carry our cross daily.

Transformation is a gradual process. We are going to experience what feel like setbacks along the way. We need to be careful not to get discouraged when things don't go the way we expect them to. Transformation is not always in a straight line. Sometimes we take a few steps backwards or sideways as we're trying to follow after Jesus. Sometimes we make a breakthrough and clear several hurdles in a row like they aren't even there. Sometimes we get scared when we realize this journey is going to be harder than we were initially thinking it would be. These are all parts of the process of growth which leads to sainthood.

Building a great relationship with someone is a process, not an event. It's not as if we can spend one weekend with someone and suddenly know every single little thing about them. We have to spend time with people over an extended period before we can say for sure we know them well and that we have a great relationship with them. In the same way, meeting Jesus and building a relationship with Him is not a one and done event. We have to put effort and attention into it if we truly want it to be something great.

God isn't afraid of our pain or sin. He wants to drive out the darkness in our life with His light and healing grace. He wants to come even into those places in our life which we consider our absolute worst. To experience the transformation He wants to work in us, though, we can't insist on hiding from Him in the dark by either refusing to admit that it is dark or insisting that we like the dark better.

We can be totally honest with God. Being honest means not only that nothing is off limits but also that we don't have to hide anything from Him. We can be angry and talk to God about our anger even if it's directed at Him. It's okay to be angry with God. It's okay to talk to God about how angry we are with Him. Our anger at God does not hurt our relationship with Him as much as staying away from God because we are angry with Him would. God isn't waiting for you to be perfect before He showers you with His love. If we were already perfect than we wouldn't need a savior, and God sent His only son to save us.

When we let God see us as we actually are instead of hiding behind a veil of perfection we are building increasing places of intimacy and trust with Him. Our relationship with Him becomes not just one where we come asking for things or only talking about the good things which are happening in our life. It becomes a relationship where we share the lows and messy places of our lives knowing God loves and cares about us enough to help us with even those places. If we only come to God with the good stuff in our life and don't talk to Him about the problems we are facing than we're shutting Him out of the very places where we need Him most. There's nothing so terrible in our lives Jesus can't handle it.

There are always places where we are not fully conformed to the perfection God is calling us to. The point is not that we never fall again. The point is that every time we fall, no matter how many times, we get back up and try again with His help. That we do not fall and then stay down in our sins preferring them to the love God is offering. Learning how to say "Yes," to keep saying "Yes," and to say an even deeper "Yes" is how we grow and mature in our relationship with Him.

Our experience of transformation may not always be comfortable, but it is worth it. It's in staying with Jesus through the ups and downs of life that we build that kind of relationship with Him where we are willing to say "Yes, I want to be with you forever in Heaven."

The road to Heaven is one we walk beside God. It is not a journey we buy a solo ticket for and then think no more about until suddenly one day we arrive after giving little thought to where we are going. It is in growing in relationship with God and allowing Him to transform us in those places we most need to be transformed that we will be ready and willing to spend forever in Heaven with Him whom we grew to know and to love here on Earth.

Ask Yourself:

1.) Do I focus more on doing things for God than doing things with God?

2.) Are you willing to be changed as a result of your relationship with Christ?

3.) What places in your life are you not willing to let God see into?

Take Action:

1.) Write down three things you would like to get better at when it comes to practicing your faith.

2.) Pick one of those three things and take a small step towards getting better at it this week. Check in at the end of the week and see how you did.

EPILOGUE

*"The world offers you comfort. But you were not
made for comfort. You were made for greatness." –
Pope Benedict XVI*

How well do you know Jesus?

That's the question we started with and it's also
the question we want to end with: How well do we
know Jesus and how well do we want to know
Him?

The thing about relationships is that they take at
least two people. A relationship won't get very far
if only one person is interested in making that
relationship work. God loves us unconditionally.
That means that there's nothing you can do which
will make God stop loving you or stop wanting to

have a relationship with you. The choice of where that relationship goes is up to you. God will not force Himself on you if you choose to ignore Him or if you push Him away.

We've talked about relationships all throughout this book. That good relationships are more than just meeting someone like it's the first time over and over again. That good relationships need communication, and that communication is a dialogue where both parties talk and not a monologue where only one person does all the talking. That it's okay to ask for things in this relationship because our asking shows where our heart is. Lastly, we talked about how great relationships don't leave you the same but transform you.

What kind of a relationship with God do you want? Do you want a relationship where you acknowledge each other from across the room? Or do you want a relationship where you live daily with Him, learning from Him and letting His love form you into the person He is inviting you to be?

Great relationships are not always easy. They are not always comfortable and they take effort and perseverance. When it comes to our relationship with God, the effort and perseverance we put forth are met and multiplied by the grace and the love of a God who has been waiting for this relationship with us since before we were born.

Would you want to spend forever with someone you hardly know?

A deeper relationship with God begins when we go from "Hi, nice to meet you!" to living in the "Now what?" "Now what?" is a daily experience of the presence of God in our lives. Not a distant God who wants to stay at arm's length but a God who loves us so much He wants to be with us forever starting not in Heaven but here and now in this very moment.

What is your response to Jesus's question to you: "Now what?"

ABOUT THE AUTHOR

Liz Garant is an accountant by day and a young adult ministry enthusiast by night. She is passionate about helping people to live their faith better. She resides in the great state of Texas. Find more of her work on Apple Podcasts for the show Catholic Immersion.

67124593R00076

Made in the USA
Lexington, KY
03 September 2017